simply casseroles

simply casseroles

Kim Lila

SURREY BOOKS

Chicago

SIMPLY CASSEROLES is published by Surrey Books, Inc.
230 E. Ohio St., Suite 120, Chicago, IL 60611

First Edition   4   5

This book is manufactured in the United States of America

Library of Congress Cataloging-in-Publication Data:

Lila, Kim.

    Simply Casseroles / by Kim Lila. — 1st ed.
    p.   cm.
    Includes index.
    ISBN 1-57284-013-7 (paper)
    1. Casserole cookery.   I. Title.
    TX693.L547   1997
    641.8'21—dc21   97-37051
                       CIP

Illustrations ©1998 Patti Green
Editorial and production: Bookcrafters, Inc., Chicago
Design and Typesetting: Joan Sommers Design, Chicago
Nutritional analyses: Linda R. Yoakam, M.S., R.D.

For free Catalog and prices on quantity purchases, contact Surrey Books at the address above

This title is distributed to the trade by Publishers Group West

First, I would like to thank my husband, Craig. He has been my greatest supporter and a devoted taste-tester. Second, and with much gratitude, I would like to thank Susan Schwartz, without whom I would not have had this opportunity.

In addition, I owe much thanks to my editor, Gene DeRoin, whose input was invaluable, to Joan Sommers for making this book a delight to see, and to Linda Yoakam for her nutritional analyses.

Lastly, I want to dedicate this, my first book, to my new son, Cole. I hope you enjoy cooking and tasting as much as your mom and dad.

contents

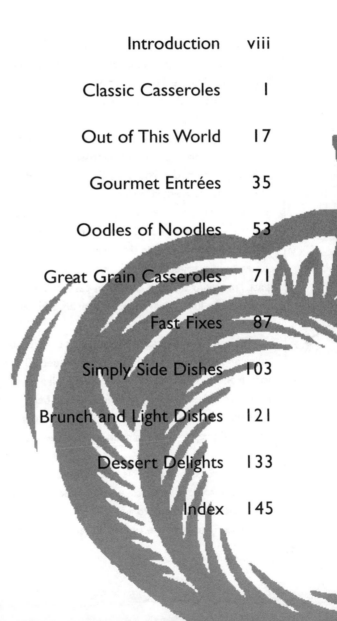

Introduction   viii

Classic Casseroles   1

Out of This World   17

Gourmet Entrées   35

Oodles of Noodles   53

Great Grain Casseroles   71

Fast Fixes   87

Simply Side Dishes   103

Brunch and Light Dishes   121

Dessert Delights   133

Index   145

introduction

Dinnertime memories—nostalgic and delicious. Warm images of family meals and hearty portions of home cooking; mother preparing grandmother's treasured recipes. But dinnertime realities are slightly different—no one has that much time for meal planning and cooking any more.

I don't believe that a busy lifestyle has to exclude the civilized pleasures of a sit-down family meal. If you want to serve your family a delicious home-cooked meal, you can. You can make a casserole, possibly in 15 minutes or less (plus baking time), team it with a salad and perhaps a side dish, and provide a complete meal that will be satisfying, interesting, nutritious, and even fun to make. *Simply Casseroles* shows you the way.

According to the Food Marketing Institute, most people eat at home five or six nights a week, and by 5:00 p.m., 70 percent of those people have no idea what they are going to put on the table that evening. Casseroles to the rescue! Not dull, tasteless leftovers bound together with cream soups—those are the ghosts of weekday dinners past. I'm talking about a variety of casserole entrées, side dishes, and even desserts that would make June Cleaver, Lucy Ricardo, and even Carol Brady give up their Ritz cracker crusts.

This new collection of classic, gourmet, ethnic, and specialty casseroles are all quick and easy to prepare; most take under 20 minutes to put together. Cooking times vary from 15 minutes to 2 hours, which leaves you free to attend to other matters or simply to relax. But saving time has not been accomplished at the expense of taste. Instead, to reduce preparation time, I have supplemented fresh ingredients with frozen items and prepared foods such as reduced-fat soups, "instant" grains, and freezer-case crusts.

Casseroles are also blessed with their own built-in time-saver. You can prepare most casseroles in advance—even a week's worth at a time—and then freeze or refrigerate them until ready to use. When that day comes, you can bring an entire meal to the table right from the oven with zero time spent on preparation.

I believe the key to casserole success is variety, so I've included a whole range of main dishes, side dishes, and desserts for you to try. Most are "kid friendly," many are suitable for casual entertaining, and they all can be the once- or twice-a-week dinner that you don't have to spend a lot of thought—or time—on.

Beginning with chapter one—"Classics"—you'll find the hearty dishes you remember Harriet cooking for Ozzie and the boys: Chicken and Dumplings, Pot Roast, Macaroni and Cheese, Turkey Pot Pie, Ham and Potato Casserole au Gratin. I've included the old-fashioned flavor but not the old-fashioned fat, slimming down these recipes and adding some of my favorite herbs and condiments to make them more interesting.

Other chapters include exciting casseroles from many lands, such as Indian Curry Chicken and Vegetables, Tamale Pie, Moussaka, Irish Stew, and seven more to make your everyday dining a little more special.

If you want to indulge in some casual entertaining, which means casual for you, too, just prepare one or two of the more glamorous casseroles ahead of time, and bake them while you and your guests are enjoying cocktails and appetizers. Your friends will love Pork Medallions with Spinach Pasta and Yogurt Sauce, Asparagus-Roughy au Gratin, Veal Scallopini, or Chicken Oscar accompanied by a fresh green salad and some crusty bread, and you'll enjoy spending the evening with them instead of in the kitchen.

When time is running out but you still want to sit down to a home-cooked meal, "Fast Fixes" will see you through the evening with 15 recipes you can make in 15 minutes or less! There's One-Dish Chicken and Rice, Italian Roll-Ups, Layered Tex-Mex Tortillas, a lightning-fast Tuna Casserole, and The Thing, a simple ground beef-mushroom soup-macaroni-green pea casserole that has been my favorite comfort food since I was three years old. Now there is no excuse for not serving your family a complete meal, unless the dog ate all your ingredients!

Because casserole cooking is so easy and convenient, I've included recipes for buffet and side-dish casseroles like Corn Bread, Baked Taco Dip, Artichokes Parmesan,

Scalloped Potatoes, and 10 more that you can make right in a baking dish. You'll also want to try the easy breakfast and brunch casseroles and the delightful dessert casseroles like Raspberry-Hazelnut Ladyfingers, Cherry Strudel, and Pear Pot Pie.

Casseroles are quick to prepare, easy to serve, and economical—the perfect mealtime solution. I hope you enjoy eating them as much as we do, and have as much fun making them as I did for this book.

Kim Lila
Chicago, Illinois

A Word About the Nutritional Data

Specific nutritional information is provided for each recipe in this book, but please remember that such data are rarely, if ever, infallible. The recipe analyses were derived using software highly regarded by nutritionists and dietitians. Figures are based on actual lab values of ingredients rather than general rules of thumb, so our results might vary slightly from traditional formulas.

Other factors affecting the nutritional data include: the variable sizes of vegetables, fruits, and cuts of meat; a plus or minus 20 percent error factor on the nutritional labels of packaged foods; and cooking techniques and appliances. Thus, if you have any health problems that mandate strict dietary requirements, it is important to consult a physician, clinical dietitian, or nutritionist before using any recipe in this book. Also, if you are a diabetic or require a diet that restricts calories, fat, or sodium, remember that the nutritional data may be accurate for the recipe we tested but not for the food you cooked due to the variables.

Please also note that ingredients listed as "optional," "to taste," or as "garnish" are not included in the nutritional data. When alternate choices of ingredients or quantities are given, the first-listed choice is the one used for the nutritional analysis. Note too that where a range is given for the number of servings that a recipe will yield ("Serves 6–8") the first, or smaller, number of servings was used to develop the "per serving" nutritional data. Thus, if more but smaller portions are served, the nutritional quantities per serving will be reduced.

classic
casseroles

Chicken and Dumplings

Porcupine Peppers

Shepherd's Pie

Chicken Divan

Pot Roast

Macaroni and Cheese

Turkey Pot Pie

Meaty Lasagne

Corned Beef and Cabbage

Chili con Carne

Ham and Potato Casserole au Gratin

classic casseroles

CHICKEN AND DUMPLINGS

Just like mom used to make—almost. This variation of an old-fashioned favorite tastes like it used to but gives you much more free time once the dish is in the oven.

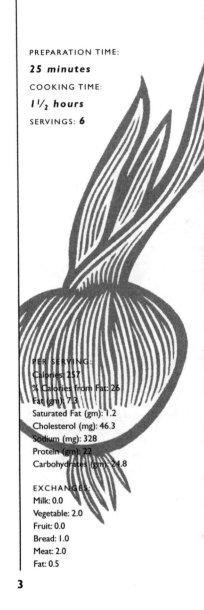

PREPARATION TIME:

25 minutes

COOKING TIME:

1 1/2 hours

SERVINGS: **6**

Vegetable cooking spray
1/2 cup skim milk
2 tablespoons light vegetable oil
1 cup flour
2 teaspoons baking powder
1/4 teaspoon salt
6 boneless, skinless chicken breast halves, uncooked
1 medium onion, finely chopped
2 celery stalks, coarsely chopped
1 10-ounce package frozen sliced carrots
1/2 teaspoon dried, crushed sage
1/4 teaspoon ground white pepper
2 13¾-ounce cans low-sodium chicken broth

Preheat oven to 325 degrees.

Coat a 2½-quart casserole with cooking spray.

In a medium bowl, combine milk and oil. Gradually stir in flour, baking powder, and salt. Mix well into a doughy consistency and set aside.

Place chicken breasts in bottom of casserole. Cover chicken with onion, celery, and carrots. Evenly sprinkle sage and pepper over vegetables; pour broth over dish.

Using the dough mixture, form 2-inch balls and drop into casserole.

Cover tightly and bake for 1½ hours.

PER SERVING:
Calories: 257
% Calories from Fat: 26
Fat (gm): 7.3
Saturated Fat (gm): 1.2
Cholesterol (mg): 46.3
Sodium (mg): 328
Protein (gm): 22
Carbohydrates (gm): 24.8

EXCHANGES:
Milk: 0.0
Vegetable: 2.0
Fruit: 0.0
Bread: 1.0
Meat: 2.0
Fat: 0.5

PORCUPINE PEPPERS

This dish is so named because the rice and meat mixture has a texture reminiscent of a porcupine—but it isn't prickly, just tasty.

PREPARATION TIME:

20 minutes

COOKING TIME:

45 minutes

SERVINGS: *4*

1 pound lean ground beef

1 14½-ounce can diced tomatoes, partially drained

2 cups uncooked minute, *or* boil-in-bag, rice

¼ teaspoon paprika

¼ teaspoon celery salt

½ teaspoon Worcestershire sauce

4 large green bell peppers, seeded

Preheat oven to 350 degrees.

Lightly coat a 9 x 9-inch glass baking dish with cooking spray, or use an uncoated, non-stick metal baking dish.

In a large mixing bowl, combine ground beef, diced tomatoes, rice, paprika, celery salt, and Worcestershire sauce. Mix with a large spoon until well blended; set aside.

Cut peppers, from top to bottom, into 4 or 5 large strips. Place half the peppers on the bottom of the baking dish. Spoon half the meat mixture, spreading evenly, over peppers. Repeat with remaining peppers and meat mixture.

Cover and bake for 45 minutes.

PER SERVING:
Calories: 441
% Calories from Fat: 32
Fat (gm): 15.4
Saturated Fat (gm): 5.9
Cholesterol (mg): 69.9
Sodium (mg): 374
Protein (gm): 25.2
Carbohydrates (gm): 49.3

EXCHANGES:
Milk: 0.0
Vegetable: 2.0
Fruit: 0.0
Bread: 2.5
Meat: 3.0
Fat: 1.0

SHEPHERD'S PIE

This classic dish can be made using leftover vegetables, meat, or mashed potatoes, making it even quicker and easier to prepare. You won't have to reheat meat or veggies; just add the recommended spices, top with mashed potatoes, and bake for the same period of time.

PREPARATION TIME:

20 minutes

COOKING TIME

35 minutes

SERVINGS: **6 – 8**

 1   pound lean ground beef
 1   large onion, finely chopped
 1   celery stalk, finely chopped
 1   teaspoon minced garlic
 1   15-ounce can tomato sauce
 1   16-ounce package mixed frozen vegetables (corn, green beans, carrots, or any other variety)
 2   bay leaves
 1   teaspoon dried thyme
 1   teaspoon dried marjoram
 $\frac{1}{4}$ teaspoon black pepper, freshly ground, if possible

MASHED POTATOES

 4   large potatoes, peeled and cut into 1-inch cubes
 1   tablespoon margarine
 $\frac{1}{4}$ cup skim milk
     Paprika, to taste

Preheat oven to 350 degrees.

In a large saute pan or skillet, add ground beef, onion, celery, and garlic; cook over medium heat until meat is browned; drain liquid. Do not return to heat.

Stir in tomato sauce, vegetables, bay leaves, thyme, marjoram, and black pepper.

MASHED POTATOES: Boil potatoes over high heat until soft; drain. Add margarine and gradually add milk while mashing potatoes with electric mixer or hand masher. The consistency of mashed potatoes should be firm; add milk, as necessary, but remember not to make the potatoes too runny. Set aside.

Transfer meat and vegetable mixture to a 2–2$\frac{1}{2}$-quart casserole. Evenly top with mashed potatoes. Sprinkle with paprika. Cover and bake for 20 minutes; uncover and bake for an additional 15 minutes or until potatoes are lightly browned.

PER SERVING:
Calories: 328
% Calories from Fat: 33
Fat (gm): 12
Saturated Fat (gm): 4.1
Cholesterol (mg): 46.8
Sodium (mg): 535
Protein (gm): 19
Carbohydrates (gm): 36.7

EXCHANGES:
Milk: 0.0
Vegetable: 2.0
Fruit: 0.0
Bread: 1.5
Meat: 2.0
Fat: 1.0

CHICKEN DIVAN

By using pre-cooked roasted chicken breast, from your grocer's meat section, and frozen broccoli, much time is saved without sacrificing flavor in this classic favorite. To save even more time, substitute cream of chicken soup for the first three ingredients, and simply add cheese to make the sauce. This dish can be prepared ahead of time and refrigerated, but add 10 minutes to cooking time. You can even freeze this dish for future use; thaw in the refrigerator before cooking.

PREPARATION TIME:

15 minutes

COOKING TIME:

35 minutes

SERVINGS: *6 – 8*

Vegetable cooking spray
- ½ cup light mayonnaise, *or* salad dressing
- ¼ cup flour
- 2½ cups skim milk
- 1 cup (4-ounce package) shredded reduced-fat sharp Cheddar cheese
- 1 2-cup package minute, *or* boil-in-bag, rice, cooked and drained
- 1 16-ounce package frozen broccoli cuts, thawed and drained
- ½ cup grated Parmesan cheese
- 1 pound roasted chicken breast, cut into ¼-inch slices

Preheat oven to 375 degrees.

In medium saucepan, whisk together salad dressing and flour over low heat until smooth. Gradually add milk, stirring constantly over medium heat until thickened. Add Cheddar cheese; stir until melted. Remove sauce from heat.

Coat a 12 x 8-inch baking dish with cooking spray. Layer rice and broccoli; top with half the sauce. Sprinkle with half the Parmesan cheese.

Top with chicken, remaining sauce, and remaining Parmesan cheese.

Bake 35 minutes or until sauce is bubbling.

PER SERVING:
Calories: 483
% Calories from Fat: 32
Fat (gm): 16.9
Saturated Fat (gm): 5.4
Cholesterol (mg): 89.1
Sodium (mg): 558
Protein (gm): 38.8
Carbohydrates (gm): 42.5

EXCHANGES:
Milk: 0.0
Vegetable: 1.0
Fruit: 0.0
Bread: 2.5
Meat: 4.0
Fat: 1.0

POT ROAST

Using fresh vegetables really makes this all-time family favorite taste great. You can use frozen vegetables if necessary, but add them during the last 45 minutes of cooking so they will not get soggy. This dish just needs to take its time cooking, so there are no real short cuts.

2–3 pound pot roast, brisket, or rump roast, fat trimmed
$\frac{1}{2}$ cup flour, divided
$\frac{1}{2}$ teaspoon black pepper, freshly ground, if possible
 1 3-pound bag baby red potatoes, washed, skins on
 4 fresh carrots, peeled, cut into 2-inch pieces
 2 medium onions, ends sliced off, cut into large pieces lengthwise
 1 8-ounce package mushrooms, rinsed, whole
 1 teaspoon dried marjoram
 1 $13\frac{3}{4}$-ounce can low-sodium, fat-free beef broth

Preheat oven to 300 degrees.

Use a large roasting pan with lid or a 13 x 9-inch, or larger, baking dish with enough foil to cover

Place meat in roaster or baking dish. Cover with half of flour, sprinkle with pepper, and pat into meat.

Place potatoes, carrots, onions, and mushrooms around meat, mixing the vegetables so flavors will blend as the dish cooks.

Sprinkle marjoram over the dish, and pour broth on top.

Cover and bake for 3 hours, basting occasionally.

GRAVY: Remove meat and vegetables from pan at the end of cooking time. Spoon off fat and discard. Place pan on stove top over medium heat.

Mix remaining flour with $\frac{1}{4}$ cup of water. Add to juices in pan and stir constantly until thickened. Season to taste with salt and pepper, if desired.

PER SERVING:
Calories: 543
% Calories from Fat: 24
Fat (gm): 14.7
Saturated Fat (gm): 3.6
Cholesterol (mg): 81.9
Sodium (mg): 105
Protein (gm): 33.4
Carbohydrates (gm): 70.2

EXCHANGES:
Milk: 0.0
Vegetable: 2.0
Fruit: 0.0
Bread: 4.0
Meat: 4.0
Fat: 0.0

MACARONI AND CHEESE

Definitely not from a box! Using reduced-fat cheeses and skim milk makes this classic favorite a somewhat lower-calorie dish packed with the creamy texture and flavor everyone loves. This is a meal by itself or a side dish for a large buffet. This casserole can be prepared ahead of time and put in the refrigerator or freezer. Cook refrigerated casserole for an additional 5 minutes (if frozen, thaw in refrigerator before cooking).

PREPARATION TIME:

10 minutes

COOKING TIME:

40 minutes

SERVINGS: **4 – 6**

Vegetable cooking spray
$\frac{1}{2}$ cup (1 stick) margarine
3 tablespoons flour
3 cups skim milk
2 cups (8-ounce package) shredded reduced-fat Cheddar cheese
$\frac{1}{4}$ cup fat-free cream cheese, softened
1 16-ounce package elbow macaroni, cooked
Paprika, to taste

Preheat oven to 350 degrees.

Coat a $2\frac{1}{2}$-quart casserole with cooking spray.

In a medium saucepan over medium heat, melt margarine. Reduce to low heat; add flour and stir until blended. Gradually stir in milk; add Cheddar and cream cheese, continuing to stir until blended and thick.

Place cooked macaroni in casserole and pour cheese mixture over top. Stir to mix well. Sprinkle with paprika.

Cover and bake for 25 minutes; uncover and bake an additional 15 minutes or until top is browned.

PER SERVING:
Calories: 760
% Calories from Fat: 26
Fat (gm): 21.7
Saturated Fat (gm): 6.5
Cholesterol (mg): 33.4
Sodium (mg): 1217
Protein (gm): 35.5
Carbohydrates (gm): 102.6

EXCHANGES:
Milk: 1.0
Vegetable: 0.0
Fruit: 0.0
Bread: 6.0
Meat: 2.0
Fat: 3.0

TURKEY POT PIE

This updated version of the classic chicken pot pie has all the flavor but is easy and quick to prepare. To save time, I use frozen puff pastry sheets from the freezer section at the grocer (there are two sheets in a box). Don't be intimidated; puff pastry sheets are easy to work with. You can use a pre-formed crust, but I find the type of crust that is unfolded and formed into a baking dish has a much better flavor.

PREPARATION TIME:
35 minutes
COOKING TIME:
55 minutes
SERVINGS: *6 – 8*

PIE CRUST

2 frozen puff pastry sheets, thawed for 20 minutes at room temperature
1 whole egg, lightly beaten, divided

FILLING

1 15-ounce jar low-sodium turkey gravy
1 teaspoon dried, crushed sage
$\frac{1}{2}$ teaspoon celery salt
$\frac{1}{4}$ teaspoon black pepper, freshly ground, if possible
1 bay leaf
1 1-pound package sliced turkey breast, cut into strips, cooked *(see Note)*
1 16-ounce package frozen mixed vegetables (any variety that you like)

Preheat oven to 400 degrees.

PIE CRUST: Unfold one pastry sheet, smooth out with wet fingertips, roll out, and mold to fit bottom of 2-quart oval, or 13 x 9-inch, casserole. Cut three 2-inch slits in crust to let out steam, otherwise crust will get soggy. Brush with beaten egg. Bake for 15 minutes or until browned. Remove from oven and set aside. Crust will be puffed, but it will deflate a little as it cools. Reduce oven to 350 degrees.

FILLING: In a medium saucepan, mix gravy with sage, celery salt, pepper, and bay leaf. Over medium heat, stir until bubbling. Remove from heat.

Add turkey strips and frozen vegetables to gravy; stir until well coated. Pour mixture into crust-lined casserole. Crust does not have to be completely cooled before pouring in turkey and vegetable mixture.

Unfold other pastry sheet, smooth out with wet fingertips, and place over filled casserole. Tuck excess pastry inside dish; do not mold around top. With a sharp knife, put three 2-inch slits on each hemisphere of crust to let steam escape. Brush with beaten egg.

Bake, uncovered, for 30 minutes. Increase oven temperature to 400 degrees and continue to bake for an additional 10 minutes or until crust is golden brown. Let casserole cool for 5 minutes before serving.

Note: A quick method of cooking turkey breast strips is to microwave them on one side for 2 minutes on high. Stir meat, turn dish, and cook on high for 3 additional minutes. Add another minute if you feel turkey isn't cooked through—microwave cooking times do vary.

PER SERVING:
Calories: 298
% Calories from Fat: 33
Fat (gm): 10.7
Saturated Fat (gm): 2.1
Cholesterol (mg): 125.5
Sodium (mg): 648
Protein (gm): 27.5
Carbohydrates (gm): 21.3

EXCHANGES:
Milk: 0.0
Vegetable: 2.0
Fruit: 0.0
Bread: 0.5
Meat: 3.0
Fat: 1.0

MEATY LASAGNE

Using sauce from a jar and adding additional spices and tomatoes enables you to make this dish quickly and avoid hours of cooking the old-fashioned way—yet retaining that same Old-World Italian flavor.

PREPARATION TIME:
20 minutes
COOKING TIME:
45 minutes
SERVINGS: **8**

Vegetable cooking spray
1 pound lean ground beef
1 teaspoon minced garlic
1 28-ounce jar spaghetti sauce, herb, mushroom, *or* any flavor you like
1 14½-ounce can diced tomatoes, drained
1 6-ounce can tomato paste
½ teaspoon each: dried basil, oregano, marjoram, parsley, *or* 2 teaspoons pre-blended Italian seasonings
1 16-ounce container reduced-fat ricotta cheese, room temperature
2 cups (8-ounce package) shredded reduced-fat mozzarella cheese, divided
2 tablespoons Parmesan cheese, divided
1 16-ounce package lasagne noodles, uncooked

Preheat oven to 325 degrees.

Coat a 13 x 9-inch glass baking dish with cooking spray.

In a large saucepan or pot, cook ground beef and garlic over medium heat until meat is browned; drain liquid.

Add spaghetti sauce, diced tomatoes, and tomato paste, cooking over low heat and stirring until mixed. Stir in spices and cook an additional 5 minutes.

In a medium bowl, combine ricotta, half of mozzarella, and half of Parmesan cheeses, mixing until well blended.

Place 3 uncooked lasagne noodles lengthwise on bottom of baking dish; break a noodle in half and set it at end of dish to fill entire length. Spread 1/3 of ricotta mixture over noodles. Using a large ladle, spoon 1/4 of meat sauce over cheese. Repeat layers two more times, alternating the pattern of noodles. Top the last cheese/sauce layer with noodles (there may be a few noodles left over) and remaining meat sauce.

Bake, uncovered, for 35 minutes. Sprinkle on the remaining mozzarella and Parmesan cheese, and continue to bake for 10 minutes or until cheese is bubbly and browned.

PER SERVING:
Calories: 454
% Calories from Fat: 32
Fat (gm): 16.4
Saturated Fat (gm): 3.3
Cholesterol (mg): 54.1
Sodium (mg): 820
Protein (gm): 30.8
Carbohydrates (gm): 47.3
EXCHANGES:
Milk: 0.0
Vegetable: 3.0
Fruit: 0.0
Bread: 2.0
Meat: 3.0
Fat: 1.5

CORNED BEEF AND CABBAGE

A favorite dish for St. Patrick's Day that can be prepared ahead of time and refrigerated. There is no need to increase the cooking time.

Vegetable cooking spray
2½ pounds lean corned beef brisket (pre-packaged in the meat section)
4 medium potatoes, peeled and quartered
1 head cabbage, rinsed and cut into 1-inch wedges
3 carrots, peeled and cut into 2-inch pieces
2 medium onions, ends sliced off and cut into large pieces lengthwise
1½ teaspoons coriander seeds
1½ teaspoons ground cloves
1½ teaspoons ground ginger
1½ cups water

Preheat oven to 325 degrees.

Use a roasting pan with lid; if unavailable, use a 13 x 9-inch baking dish with enough foil to cover. Coat bottom of pan with cooking spray.

Place corned beef in pan. Place potatoes, cabbage, carrots, and onions around the meat, mixing vegetables so the flavors will blend as the dish cooks.

In a small bowl, combine coriander seeds, ground cloves, and ground ginger. Stir until mixed well. Sprinkle evenly over meat and vegetables.

Slowly pour water over entire pan.

Cover and bake for 2 hours, basting occasionally.

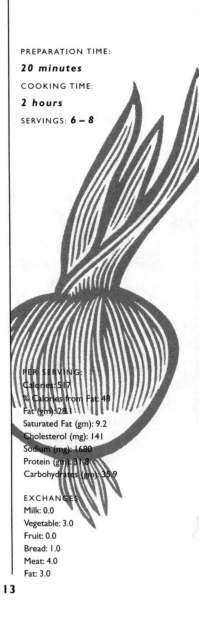

PREPARATION TIME:
20 minutes
COOKING TIME:
2 hours
SERVINGS: *6 – 8*

PER SERVING:
Calories: 517
% Calories from Fat: 48
Fat (gm): 28.1
Saturated Fat (gm): 9.2
Cholesterol (mg): 141
Sodium (mg): 1680
Protein (gm): 31.8
Carbohydrates (gm): 35.9

EXCHANGES:
Milk: 0.0
Vegetable: 3.0
Fruit: 0.0
Bread: 1.0
Meat: 4.0
Fat: 3.0

CHILI CON CARNE

Try topping this well-known favorite with reduced-fat Cheddar cheese, onions, and/or fat-free sour cream for variety.

PREPARATION TIME:
25 minutes

COOKING TIME:
$1\frac{1}{4}$ hours

SERVINGS: **6 – 8**

1 pound beef round, *or* skirt, steak, fat trimmed, cut into 1-inch pieces
1 teaspoon minced garlic
1 large onion, finely chopped
1 large green bell pepper, seeded and finely chopped
1 large red bell pepper, seeded and finely chopped
1 large yellow bell pepper, seeded and finely chopped
1 large banana pepper, seeded and finely chopped
1 large jalapeño pepper, finely chopped (for spicier chili, use 2 peppers)
1 $14\frac{1}{2}$-ounce can diced tomatoes, undrained
1 15-ounce can tomato sauce
1 6-ounce can tomato paste
1 $15\frac{1}{2}$-ounce can light red kidney beans, drained
1 $15\frac{1}{2}$-ounce can dark red kidney beans, drained
1 teaspoon chili powder
1 teaspoon cumin powder
1 bay leaf

Preheat oven to 350 degrees.

Combine meat with garlic in a large saute pan or skillet and cook over medium heat until meat is browned; drain liquid.

Add onion, all of the peppers, diced tomatoes, tomato sauce and paste, and light and dark kidney beans to the meat. Stir until well mixed; add spices.

Pour mixture into a $2\frac{1}{2}$-quart casserole. Cover and bake for 1 hour and 15 minutes. Serve with garnishes such as cheese, onions, or sour cream.

PER SERVING:
Calories: 306
% Calories from Fat: 11
Fat (gm): 4.4
Saturated Fat (gm): 0.9
Cholesterol (mg): 36.5
Sodium (mg): 1081
Protein (gm): 29.3
Carbohydrates (gm): 48.9

EXCHANGES:
Milk: 0.0
Vegetable: 3.0
Fruit: 0.0
Bread: 2.0
Meat: 2.0
Fat: 0.0

HAM AND POTATO CASSEROLE AU GRATIN

Another old-fashioned casserole modified to meet today's healthy standards while retaining that nostalgic flavor.

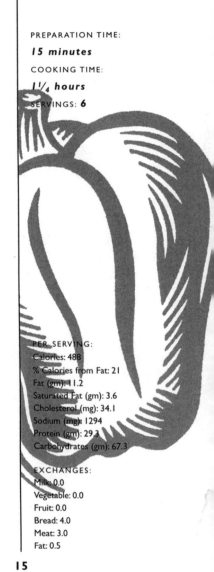

Vegetable cooking spray

6 large red potatoes, peeled and thinly sliced, divided

1 pound cooked lean ham, cut into 1-inch cubes

1 small green bell pepper, seeded and finely chopped

3 scallions, finely chopped (include some green tops)

1 cup (4-ounce package) shredded reduced-fat Cheddar cheese

2 tablespoons margarine

3 tablespoons flour

¾ teaspoon powdered mustard

2 cups skim milk

⅛ teaspoon black pepper, freshly ground, if possible

¼ teaspoon paprika

½ cup unseasoned breadcrumbs

Preheat oven to 375 degrees.

Coat a 2-quart casserole with cooking spray, and arrange half the sliced potatoes on the bottom, overlapping.

In a medium bowl, combine ham, bell pepper, and scallions. Evenly scatter over potatoes; top with remaining potato slices and sprinkle with cheese.

In a small saucepan, melt margarine and blend in flour and mustard. Slowly add milk and continue to stir over medium heat until sauce thickens; mix in black pepper and paprika. Pour sauce evenly over potatoes and ham.

Cover and bake for 45 minutes; uncover and continue to bake for an additional 30 minutes or until potatoes are fork-tender and golden brown.

PREPARATION TIME:
15 minutes
COOKING TIME:
1¼ hours
SERVINGS: **6**

PER SERVING:
Calories: 488
% Calories from Fat: 21
Fat (gm): 11.2
Saturated Fat (gm): 3.6
Cholesterol (mg): 34.1
Sodium (mg): 1294
Protein (gm): 29.3
Carbohydrates (gm): 67.3

EXCHANGES:
Milk: 0.0
Vegetable: 0.0
Fruit: 0.0
Bread: 4.0
Meat: 3.0
Fat: 0.5

out of
this world

Beef Enchiladas

Indian Curry Chicken and Vegetables

Tamale Pie

Hungarian Goulash

Swedish Meatballs

Cassoulet au Craig

Moussaka

Coq au Vin (Chicken in Wine)

Swiss and Spinach Quiche

Philippine Pancit

Irish Stew

out of this world

BEEF ENCHILADAS

For a meatless version of this Southwestern dish, eliminate the beef and use one cup of reduced-fat Cheddar cheese mixed with one 28-ounce can of fat-free refried beans. Chicken or shrimp can also be used instead of beef.

1 pound beef skirt, *or* flank, steak, fat trimmed, cut into 2-inch strips
1 teaspoon minced garlic
½ teaspoon chili powder
½ teaspoon ground cumin
1 tablespoon lime juice
2 cups minute, *or* boil-in-bag, rice, cooked according to package directions
1 10-ounce package frozen corn, broken apart
8 wheat flour tortillas
1 4-ounce can diced green chilies
2 cups (8-ounce package) shredded reduced-fat Cheddar cheese
1 10-ounce can enchilada sauce

GARNISHES, IF DESIRED:

Chopped jalapeños
Chopped fresh cilantro
Fat-free sour cream

Preheat oven to 325 degrees.

Combine meat with garlic in a medium saute pan or skillet and cook over medium heat until meat is browned; drain liquid. Add chili powder, cumin, and lime juice and stir until blended.

In a 2–2½-quart casserole, combine rice and frozen corn; spread evenly.

Place a few spoonfuls of meat mixture in each tortilla, roll up, and place seam side down on top of rice and corn mixture.

Top the rolled tortillas with diced green chilies and Cheddar cheese. Pour enchilada sauce over all.

Cover and bake for 50 minutes. Serve with desired garnishes.

PREPARATION TIME:
20 minutes
COOKING TIME:
50 minutes
SERVINGS: **4 – 6**

PER SERVING:
Calories: 824
% Calories from Fat: 27
Fat (gm): 24.1
Saturated Fat (gm): 9.4
Cholesterol (mg): 88.1
Sodium (mg): 1695
Protein (gm): 46.4
Carbohydrates (gm): 102

EXCHANGES:
Milk: 0.0
Vegetable: 2.0
Fruit: 0.0
Bread: 6.0
Meat: 5.0
Fat: 1.5

INDIAN CURRY CHICKEN AND VEGETABLES

Using many different vegetables gives this curry dish a variety of colors and textures. For this casserole I recommend preparing brown rice separately so it is fairly firm; however, you may cook it with the casserole (place uncooked rice in bottom of dish first) but add 20 minutes to the cooking time. If you want to save a little time, or you don't have all of the spices on hand, substitute 2½ tablespoons of curry powder for the first 7 ingredients. That will give the dish a slightly different flavor, but it will still be very tasty. Don't forget about using frozen vegetables as an additional time saver.

PREPARATION TIME:
25 minutes
COOKING TIME:
1¼ hours
SERVINGS: **4**

2 teaspoons turmeric
1 teaspoon cumin
1 teaspoon mustard seed, ground, *or* mustard powder
4 teaspoons coriander
½ teaspoon chili powder
1 teaspoon ginger
1 teaspoon black pepper, freshly ground, if possible
1 large onion, finely chopped
1 cup (8 ounces) evaporated milk
2 tablespoons white wine vinegar
1 15-ounce can crushed tomatoes, undrained
1 6-ounce can tomato paste
2 tablespoons brown sugar
1 13¾-ounce can low-sodium, fat-free vegetable broth
4 boneless, skinless chicken breast halves, cut into 1-inch pieces
1 8-ounce package mushrooms, rinsed and roughly chopped
¾ cup carrots, roughly chopped
¾ cup okra, roughly chopped
¾ cup cauliflower, roughly chopped
1 large potato, cut into 1-inch cubes

NOTE: Choose any combination of vegetables, up to 4 cups

2 cups brown long-grain rice, cooked according to package directions

20

Preheat oven to 350 degrees.

Combine all 7 spices and, if you have a grinder, grind for a few seconds. Set aside.

In a medium saucepan over low heat, combine onion, milk, vinegar, tomatoes, tomato paste, sugar, and broth. Stir until mixture is blended. Add the spices. Bring to a light boil, stirring occasionally; remove from heat.

In a large mixing bowl, combine chicken pieces and all vegetables. Transfer mixture to a large round or oval 2–2½-quart casserole dish. Pour the tomato-spice sauce evenly over vegetables and chicken. Cover tightly and bake for 1 hour and 15 minutes. Serve over cooked brown rice.

PER SERVING:
Calories: 755
% Calories from Fat: 10
Fat (gm): 8.6
Saturated Fat (gm): 2.3
Cholesterol (mg): 77.4
Sodium (mg): 703
Protein (gm): 45.6
Carbohydrates (gm): 126

EXCHANGES:
Milk: 0.5
Vegetable: 4.0
Fruit: 0.0
Bread: 7.0
Meat: 3.0
Fat: 0.0

TAMALE PIE

This casserole can easily be prepared ahead of time and refrigerated. Add 15 minutes to the cooking time to ensure that it is heated through.

1 pound lean ground beef

1 medium onion, chopped

1 garlic clove, minced

2 teaspoons chili powder

1¼ teaspoons ground cumin, divided

1 15-ounce can tomato sauce

1 4-ounce can diced green chili peppers, drained

1 cup cornmeal, yellow or white

Tabasco, *or* hot, sauce, to taste (a few drops will add zest; adjust to your taste)

2 cups water

1 tablespoon margarine

1 10-ounce package frozen corn

1 cup (4-ounce package) shredded reduced-fat Cheddar cheese

Preheat oven to 375 degrees.

Using a large saute or fry pan, cook ground beef, onion, and garlic over medium heat until beef is browned. Break-up the ground beef into small pieces as it cooks. Stir in chili powder, 1 teaspoon of ground cumin, tomato sauce, and chili peppers. Simmer over low heat, stirring occasionally, while preparing the cornmeal mixture.

In a small saucepan, combine cornmeal, remaining ground cumin, Tabasco or hot sauce, and water. Stir until blended. Bring to a boil, stir in margarine, reduce heat, and simmer until thick, 3-4 minutes.

Mix frozen corn and cheese into meat mixture, and continue to simmer for an additional minute.

Pour meat and cheese mixture into an ungreased 2-quart round or oval glass baking dish. Spoon on the cornmeal mixture and bake, uncovered, for 40 minutes or until the cornmeal is browned.

HUNGARIAN GOULASH

Serve this dish with wide noodles, either egg or no-yolk. The noodles are best when cooked separately as the length of cooking time will make them soggy. To cut cooking time to 1 hour, brown the meat before use.

Vegetable cooking spray
2 pounds round steak, fat trimmed, cut into $\frac{1}{2}$-inch cubes
1 medium onion, finely chopped
1 teaspoon minced garlic
2 tablespoons flour
$\frac{1}{2}$ teaspoon black pepper, freshly ground, if possible
$1\frac{1}{2}$ teaspoons paprika
$\frac{1}{4}$ teaspoon dried thyme
1 bay leaf
1 $14\frac{1}{2}$-ounce can diced tomatoes
1 8-ounce container fat-free sour cream
1 12-ounce package wide egg noodles, *or* no-yolk noodles, cooked

Preheat oven to 325 degrees.

Coat a $2\frac{1}{2}$-quart casserole with cooking spray.

Place steak, onion, and garlic in casserole; stir in flour to coat meat and onion.

Add pepper, paprika, thyme, bay leaf, and tomatoes; stir to blend well.

Cover and bake for $1\frac{1}{2}$ hours. Stir in sour cream and bake for an additional 30 minutes. Serve over wide noodles.

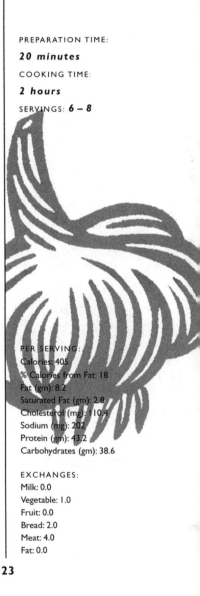

PREPARATION TIME:
20 minutes
COOKING TIME:
2 hours
SERVINGS: **6 – 8**

PER SERVING:
Calories: 405
% Calories from Fat: 18
Fat (gm): 8.2
Saturated Fat (gm): 2.8
Cholesterol (mg): 110.4
Sodium (mg): 202
Protein (gm): 43.2
Carbohydrates (gm): 38.6

EXCHANGES:
Milk: 0.0
Vegetable: 1.0
Fruit: 0.0
Bread: 2.0
Meat: 4.0
Fat: 0.0

23

SWEDISH MEATBALLS

This variation of traditional Swedish meatballs uses ground turkey in addition to lean ground beef to reduce calories and fat. This dish should be served with wide egg or no-yolk noodles. To cut cooking time in half, brown the meatballs before putting them into the casserole and cook for only 45 minutes.

PREPARATION TIME:
25 minutes
COOKING TIME:
1 1/2 hours
SERVINGS: **6 – 8**

Vegetable cooking spray

MEATBALLS

- 1 medium yellow onion, minced
- 1 tablespoon margarine
- 3/4 pound lean ground beef
- 1/2 pound ground turkey
- 1/4 teaspoon salt
- 1/4 teaspoon black pepper, freshly ground, if possible
- Pinch nutmeg
- 3/4 cup unseasoned breadcrumbs
- 1/4 cup skim milk
- 1/4 cup water
- 1 egg, lightly beaten
- 1 12-ounce package wide egg, *or* no-yolk noodles, cooked according to package directions

GRAVY

- 2 tablespoons margarine
- 2 tablespoons flour
- 1 1/4 cups skim milk
- 1/4 teaspoon paprika
- Pinch white pepper, *or* black pepper if white is unavailable

Preheat oven to 325 degrees.

Coat a 2 1/2-quart casserole with cooking spray.

24

MEATBALLS: In a small saute pan or skillet, saute onion in margarine over medium heat until onion is limp.

In a medium bowl, mix the cooked onion with all remaining ingredients for meatballs, except noodles. Shape into 1-inch balls with your hands, a better method than using a fork or spoon. Place meatballs into the casserole.

GRAVY: In a small saucepan over medium heat, melt margarine. Reduce to low heat; add flour and stir until blended. Gradually stir in milk; add paprika and pepper. Continue to stir over medium heat until thickened. Pour over meatballs.

Cover and bake for 1½ hours. Serve over wide noodles.

PER SERVING:
Calories: 474
% Calories from Fat: 39
Fat (gm): 20.2
Saturated Fat (gm): 5.9
Cholesterol (mg): 126
Sodium (mg): 376
Protein (gm): 27.4
Carbohydrates (gm): 44.2

EXCHANGES:
Milk: 0.0
Vegetable: 0.0
Fruit: 0.0
Bread: 3.0
Meat: 3.0
Fat: 2.0

CASSOULET AU CRAIG

Cassoulet, or potted meat and white beans, is a staple of French country cooking. This version has the beans but cuts out much of the fat and sodium commonly found in traditional versions of this famous dish. This variation is named after my husband—it's his favorite.

PREPARATION TIME:

25 minutes

COOKING TIME:

2 1/2 hours

SERVINGS: **8**

Vegetable cooking spray

1 pound pork loin, fat trimmed, cut into 1-inch cubes

1/2 pound lamb, fat trimmed, cut into 1-inch cubes

1 8-ounce package turkey sausage, cut into 1-inch pieces

3 slices low-sodium bacon, cut into 1-inch pieces

3 15 1/2-ounce cans Great Northern white beans, drained

4 shallots, *or* very small onions, cut in halves

2 teaspoons minced garlic

2 14 1/2-ounce cans diced tomatoes, undrained

2 6-ounce cans tomato paste

1 stalk celery, coarsely chopped

1 bay leaf

1 teaspoon dried parsley

1 teaspoon dried thyme

1 cup unseasoned breadcrumbs

PER SERVING:

Calories: 461

% Calories from Fat: 19

Fat (gm): 10.1

Saturated Fat (gm): 2.8

Cholesterol (mg): 63.7

Sodium (mg): 1278

Protein (gm): 36.2

Carbohydrates (gm): 58.4

EXCHANGES:

Milk: 0.0

Vegetable: 3.0

Fruit: 0.0

Bread: 3.0

Meat: 3.0

Fat: 0.0

Preheat oven to 325 degrees.

Coat a large roaster pan or Dutch oven (the size a turkey would be cooked in) with cooking spray.

Place pork, lamb, sausage, bacon, and beans in bottom of roaster. Randomly, place shallot halves around the meat. Sprinkle the garlic over meat and shallots.

In a medium bowl, mix tomatoes, tomato paste, celery, bay leaf, parsley, and thyme until blended; pour over meat and beans.

Evenly sprinkle breadcrumbs over the casserole.

Cover and bake for 2 hours; uncover and bake for an additional 1/2 hour. Skim any fat that rises to the top before serving.

MOUSSAKA

This classic Greek dish takes a while to prepare, but after one taste you'll find it was well worth the time. As a time saver, you can substitute canned lentils and put the potatoes in the casserole uncooked—but slice them fairly thin.

PREPARATION TIME:
45 minutes
COOKING TIME:
40 minutes
SERVINGS: **4 – 6**

1¼ cups green lentils, uncooked
1 large eggplant, cut into ¼-inch slices
4 tablespoons olive oil
1 large onion, coarsely chopped
1 teaspoon minced garlic
1 large carrot, coarsely chopped, *or* 1 cup frozen sliced carrots
4 celery stalks, finely chopped
½ teaspoon dried thyme
½ teaspoon dried parsley
1 14½-ounce can peeled tomatoes, partially drained
2 teaspoons soy sauce
Black pepper, to taste, freshly ground, if possible
2 medium potatoes, cooked and sliced
2 medium tomatoes, sliced

SAUCE

4 tablespoons margarine
4 tablespoons flour
1¾ cups skim milk
1 large egg, separated
½ cup shredded Cheddar cheese
1 teaspoon nutmeg

Preheat oven to 350 degrees.

Cook lentils in plenty of water (5 cups) until soft. Drain and reserve ½ cup of the liquid. If you decide to use canned lentils, reserve liquid from the can.

27

In a large saute pan or skillet, cook the eggplant in olive oil over medium/high heat. Remove eggplant from pan and place on paper towels to absorb some of the oil. Leave remaining oil in pan.

In that same pan, saute onion, garlic, carrot, and celery, adding the ½ cup of reserved liquid from the lentils. Over low heat, simmer, covered, until carrots are just tender, 8-10 minutes.

Continue to simmer, adding the lentils, thyme, parsley, and tomatoes. Cook for an additional 3-4 minutes. Stir in soy sauce and pepper; remove from heat.

Place a layer of the lentil mixture in a 9 x 13-inch casserole and cover with half of the eggplant slices. Cover the eggplant with half of the potato slices and all of the tomato slices. Repeat with the remaining lentils, eggplant, and potatoes.

SAUCE: In a small saucepan over medium heat, melt the margarine and reduce heat. Add flour, stirring continuously until blended; this smooth mixture is called a roux. Add milk gradually, blending well so that the sauce is smooth.

Increase heat and stir continually until sauce thickens. Remove from heat. Add egg yolk and stir in cheese and nutmeg.

Beat the egg white until stiff, using a whisk, eggbeater, or fork (peaks will begin to form as you beat), then carefully fold the stiffened egg white into the sauce.

Pour the sauce over the moussaka, covering the dish evenly and completely.

Bake, uncovered, for 40 minutes or until top is puffy and golden brown.

PER SERVING:
Calories: 820
% Calories from Fat: 39
Fat (gm): 36.1
Saturated Fat (gm): 10.3
Cholesterol (mg): 85
Sodium (mg): 1039
Protein (gm): 30.2
Carbohydrates (gm): 97.6

EXCHANGES:
Milk: 0.0
Vegetable: 4.0
Fruit: 0.0
Bread: 4.0
Meat: 2.0
Fat: 7.0

COQ AU VIN (CHICKEN IN WINE)

A French classic that can be made in advance and refrigerated. In that case, add 10 minutes to cooking time.

6 boneless, skinless chicken breast halves, cut in halves
5 slices low-sodium bacon, diced
3 green onions, sliced
5 small white onions, peeled and cut in halves
1 8-ounce package mushrooms, whole
8 small new potatoes, cleaned and cut in halves
1 teaspoon minced garlic
$\frac{1}{2}$ teaspoon salt
$\frac{1}{4}$ teaspoon pepper
$\frac{1}{2}$ teaspoon dried thyme
$\frac{1}{2}$ cup water
$\frac{1}{2}$ cup Burgundy, *or* other dry red wine
Parsley, freshly chopped for garnish, if desired

Preheat oven to 325 degrees.

In a $2\frac{1}{2}$-quart casserole, place chicken and bacon. Sprinkle green onions on top of meat. Add white onions, mushrooms, and potatoes.

In a small bowl, combine garlic, salt, pepper, and thyme. Sprinkle evenly over meat and vegetables. Pour water and wine over entire dish.

Cover and bake for $1\frac{1}{2}$ hours.

PREPARATION TIME:
25 minutes
COOKING TIME:
$1\frac{1}{2}$ hours
SERVINGS: 6

PER SERVING:
Calories: 535
% Calories from Fat: 10
Fat (gm): 6.2
Saturated Fat (gm): 1
Cholesterol (mg): 76.3
Sodium (mg): 307
Protein (gm): 35.5
Carbohydrates (gm): 81.9

EXCHANGES:
Milk: 0.0
Vegetable: 1.0
Fruit: 0.0
Bread: 4.5
Meat: 3.0
Fat: 0.0

SWISS AND SPINACH QUICHE

Something different for breakfast or a great brunch. This quiche is quick to make and leaves you hands-free to prepare any additional items, such as fresh fruit, to accompany this delicious meal.

PREPARATION TIME:
10 minutes
COOKING TIME:
40 – 50 minutes
SERVINGS: *4 – 6*

1 $7\frac{1}{2}$-ounce package buttermilk biscuits, uncooked (found in the dairy section)
4 ounces Swiss cheese, cut into strips
1 cup (4-ounce package) shredded reduced-fat mozzarella cheese
2 tablespoons flour
1 cup skim milk
3 eggs, lightly beaten
$\frac{1}{4}$ teaspoon salt
$\frac{1}{2}$ teaspoon black pepper, freshly ground if possible
$\frac{1}{4}$ teaspoon nutmeg
1 10-ounce package frozen spinach, cooked and well drained

Preheat oven to 375 degrees.

Separate biscuits and place in an ungreased 8- or 9-inch pie pan or quiche dish; press edges of biscuits together to line the pan and sides.

In a medium bowl, toss Swiss and mozzarella cheese with flour; arrange evenly over biscuits.

Using same bowl, mix milk, eggs, salt, pepper, nutmeg, and spinach until blended.

Pour over cheese and bake for 40-50 minutes or until golden brown. Serve warm.

Note: To lower calories and fat, use reduced-fat mozzarella cheese and egg substitute. These substitutes will also reduce the cholesterol.

PER SERVING:
Calories: 411
% Calories from Fat: 41
Fat (gm): 18.8
Saturated Fat (gm): 9.2
Cholesterol (mg): 202.7
Sodium (mg): 910
Protein (gm): 26.1
Carbohydrates (gm): 36

EXCHANGES:
Milk: 0.0
Vegetable: 0.0
Fruit: 0.0
Bread: 2.0
Meat: 3.0
Fat: 2.0

PHILIPPINE PANCIT

Pancit is a traditional noodle dish with many variations. You can add other vegetables or meats that may be leftover from another meal to create your own version of this Philippine favorite. This dish can be prepared ahead of time and refrigerated, but in that case add the noodles uncooked and increase cooking time by 15 minutes.

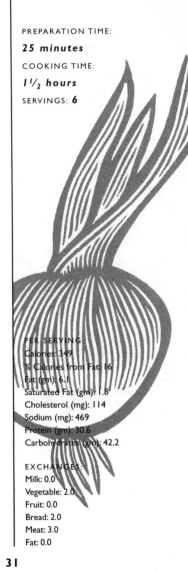

PREPARATION TIME:
25 minutes
COOKING TIME:
1 1/2 hours
SERVINGS: **6**

- 3/4 pound lean boneless pork, cut into 1-inch strips
- 1 boneless, skinless, whole chicken breast, cut into 1/2-inch strips
- 1 12-ounce package thin egg noodles, cooked *al dente*
- 2 teaspoons minced garlic
- 1 small onion, coarsely chopped
- 2 large carrots, coarsely shredded
- 2 celery stalks, thinly sliced, diagonally
- 1 10-ounce package frozen lima beans, thawed and drained
- 1/2 cup water
- 1 tablespoon paprika
- 1/4 pound shrimp, shelled, deveined, and cut in halves
- 3 tablespoons fish sauce (you can find small bottles in the ethnic aisle)

Preheat oven to 325 degrees.

Place pork and chicken strips in a large roasting pan or Dutch oven (the size a turkey would be cooked in); cover with noodles.

In a small bowl, combine garlic, onion, carrots, celery, lima beans, and water. Pour evenly over noodles. Sprinkle paprika over all.

Scatter shrimp pieces over entire dish and evenly pour fish sauce on top.

Cover and bake for 1 1/2 hours.

PER SERVING:
Calories: 349
% Calories from Fat: 16
Fat (gm): 6.1
Saturated Fat (gm): 1.8
Cholesterol (mg): 114
Sodium (mg): 469
Protein (gm): 30.6
Carbohydrates (gm): 42.2

EXCHANGES:
Milk: 0.0
Vegetable: 2.0
Fruit: 0.0
Bread: 2.0
Meat: 3.0
Fat: 0.0

IRISH STEW

If you want to reduce cooking time, brown the meat before proceeding with casserole, and then cook for only 1 hour.

Vegetable cooking spray
2 pounds boneless lamb, cut into 1-inch cubes
$\frac{1}{4}$ teaspoon salt
$\frac{1}{4}$ teaspoon pepper
1 bay leaf
4 medium potatoes, peeled and quartered
3 medium carrots, peeled and cut into $\frac{1}{2}$-inch slices
2 small onions, thinly sliced
$\frac{1}{4}$ cup quick-cooking tapioca (to thicken stew)
1 10-ounce package frozen peas, *or* other vegetable
2 cups water

Preheat oven to 325 degrees.

Coat a $2\frac{1}{2}$-quart casserole with cooking spray.

Season cubed lamb with salt and pepper; place in casserole and mix in bay leaf, potatoes, carrots, onions, tapioca, and peas. Pour water over top.

Cover and bake for 1 hour; stir ingredients and return to oven for an additional hour.

COOKING TIME:
2 hours
SERVINGS: **6 – 8**

PER SERVING:
Calories: 464
% Calories from Fat: 22
Fat (gm): 11.1
Saturated Fat (gm): 3.9
Cholesterol (mg): 104
Sodium (mg): 239
Protein (gm): 38.1
Carbohydrates (gm): 52.4

EXCHANGES:
Milk: 0.0
Vegetable: 1.0
Fruit: 0.0
Bread: 3.0
Meat: 4.0
Fat: 0.0

gourmet entrées

Spinach Soufflé

Salmon Casserole

Chicken Oscar

Spinach-Stuffed Shells

Layered Eggplant and Zucchini Bake

Veal Scallopini

Stir-Fry Fish and Vegetable Bake

Chicken Stuffed with Vegetables

Pork Medallions with Spinach Pasta and Yogurt Sauce

Shish-Kabob Casserole

Asparagus-Roughy au Gratin

Salmon, Pea Pod, and New Potato Casserole

Pork Tenderloin with Apricot Stuffing

Salmon Soufflé

g o u r m e t   e n t r é e s

SPINACH SOUFFLÉ

Use fresh, frozen, or leftover spinach (or other vegetable) in soufflé, but drain very well before chopping and measuring so sauce will remain thick. Serve this dish immediately after removing from the oven as it loses its height as it cools. An excellent accompaniment to this light meal is a tossed salad with many vegetables and a light vinaigrette dressing.

PREPARATION TIME:

15 minutes

COOKING TIME:

35 – 45 minutes

SERVINGS: *4*

Vegetable cooking spray
2 tablespoons margarine
1 small white onion, minced
3 tablespoons flour
½ teaspoon ground nutmeg
½ cup light cream
½ cup beef broth
4 eggs, separated; yolks lightly beaten
Pinch white pepper
1 10-ounce package frozen spinach, thawed, well drained and finely chopped
Pinch cream of tartar

Preheat oven to 350 degrees.

Heavily coat an 8-inch soufflé dish, or straight-sided cake pan, with cooking spray.

Melt margarine in a medium saucepan over medium heat. Blend in onion, flour, and nutmeg; slowly stir in cream and broth. Continue to stir over heat until thickened, 3-5 minutes.

Reduce to low heat and stir in egg yolks, cooking for 1-2 minutes. Remove from heat.

Mix in pepper and spinach. Cool to room temperature.

Using an electric mixer, beat egg whites until frothy; add cream of tartar, and continue beating until stiff but not dry. Fold whites into spinach mixture; spoon into soufflé dish.

Bake, uncovered, for 35-45 minutes or until puffy and browned. Serve at once.

PER SERVING:
Calories: 232
% Calories from Fat: 64
Fat (gm): 16.7
Saturated Fat (gm): 6.4
Cholesterol (mg): 233
Sodium (mg): 387
Protein (gm): 10.2
Carbohydrates (gm): 10.9

EXCHANGES:
Milk: 0.0
Vegetable: 1.0
Fruit: 0.0
Bread: 0.5
Meat: 1.0
Fat: 3.0

SALMON CASSEROLE

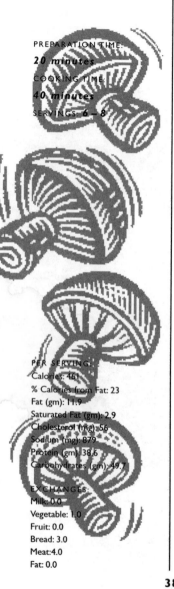

This light and flavorful casserole is great for brunch, lunch, or dinner.

PREPARATION TIME:
20 minutes
COOKING TIME:
40 minutes
SERVINGS *6 – 8*

Vegetable cooking spray
2 14¾-ounce cans boneless salmon, flaked (it may be necessary to remove bones)
¼ teaspoon black pepper, freshly ground, if possible
½ teaspoon ground nutmeg
1 16-ounce package mushrooms, rinsed and coarsely chopped
3 tablespoons light margarine
2 tablespoons (heaping) flour
1½ cups skim milk
1 shallot, finely chopped
2 whole cloves
1 bay leaf
½ cup unseasoned breadcrumbs
4 potatoes, peeled, boiled, and mashed
1 teaspoon paprika

Preheat oven to 375 degrees.

Coat a 12 x 8-inch casserole with cooking spray.

Combine salmon, pepper, nutmeg, and mushrooms in casserole.

In a small saucepan, melt margarine over low heat. Remove from heat; add flour, stir until smooth, and return to heat. Slowly stir in milk; add shallot, cloves, and bay leaf and continue to cook for 2-3 minutes, stirring occasionally.

Remove cloves and pour sauce over salmon.

Cover top evenly with breadcrumbs. Place mashed potatoes around border of dish and sprinkle with paprika.

Bake, uncovered, for 35-40 minutes or until top is lightly browned.

PER SERVING:
Calories: 461
% Calories from Fat: 23
Fat (gm): 11.9
Saturated Fat (gm): 2.9
Cholesterol (mg): 56
Sodium (mg): 879
Protein (gm): 38.6
Carbohydrates (gm): 49.7
EXCHANGES:
Milk: 0.0
Vegetable: 1.0
Fruit: 0.0
Bread: 3.0
Meat: 4.0
Fat: 0.0

CHICKEN OSCAR

This dish is easy to prepare and looks great when presented.

Vegetable cooking spray
6 boneless, skinless chicken breast halves
1 cup unseasoned breadcrumbs, in zip-style bag
2 cups seasoned bread cubes, *or* stuffing
$\frac{1}{2}$ cup low-sodium, fat-free chicken broth
24 stalks asparagus
6 slices ($\frac{1}{8}$ inch thick) provolone cheese

Preheat oven to 350 degrees.

Lightly coat a 13 x 9-inch baking dish with cooking spray.

Place each chicken breast between waxed paper. Using a mallet or large wooden spoon, pound to about $\frac{1}{4}$ inch thickness. Remove paper.

Put one chicken breast half in the zip-style bag containing breadcrumbs and shake until breast is coated. Repeat for each chicken breast. Place in the baking dish.

In a medium mixing bowl, combine the bread cubes and broth, mixing gently until bread cubes are moist. Spoon equal amounts onto the center of each chicken breast.

Cut off the bottom two inches of asparagus stalks. Place 2 stalks abreast and 2 stalks crisscross on each chicken breast.

Top each breast with a slice of provolone cheese.

Cover and bake for 30 minutes; uncover and bake for an additional 10 minutes.

PREPARATION TIME:
20 minutes
COOKING TIME:
40 minutes
SERVINGS: **6**

PER SERVING:
Calories: 474
% Calories from Fat: 25
Fat (gm): 12.8
Saturated Fat (gm): 6.2
Cholesterol (mg): 93
Sodium (mg): 1555
Protein (gm): 44
Carbohydrates (gm): 43.7

EXCHANGES:
Milk: 0.0
Vegetable: 0.0
Fruit: 0.0
Bread: 3.0
Meat: 4.0
Fat: 1.0

SPINACH-STUFFED SHELLS

Using frozen spinach and jarred sauce is a real time saver for this delicious dish.

PREPARATION TIME:
20 minutes
COOKING TIME:
40 minutes
SERVINGS: **6**

PER SERVING:
Calories: 449
% Calories from Fat: 16
Fat (gm): 8.1
Saturated Fat (gm): 5.1
Cholesterol (mg): 23.5
Sodium (mg): 962
Protein (gm): 33.6
Carbohydrates (gm): 61.9

EXCHANGES:
Milk: 0.0
Vegetable: 0.0
Fruit: 0.0
Bread: 4.0
Meat: 3.0
Fat: 0.0

1 16-ounce container fat-free ricotta cheese
2 cups shredded reduced-fat mozzarella cheese, divided
2 teaspoons dried basil, divided
2 teaspoons dried oregano, divided
2 teaspoons minced garlic, divided
1 10-ounce package frozen cut spinach, thawed and drained
1 14½-ounce can diced tomatoes, drained
1 15-ounce can tomato sauce
¼ cup grated Parmesan cheese
1 12-ounce package extra-large pasta shells, cooked *al dente*
1 teaspoon dried parsley

Preheat oven to 325 degrees.

In a medium bowl, combine ricotta cheese, half of the mozzarella cheese, and 1 teaspoon each of the basil, oregano, and garlic. Add the spinach and mix well. Set aside.

In a medium bowl, combine tomatoes, tomato sauce, Parmesan cheese, and the remaining basil, oregano, and garlic. Set aside.

Stuff each shell, until over-filled, with the cheese and spinach mixture (you may run out of mixture before shells). Set shells closely together in a 13 x 9-inch baking dish.

Spoon tomato mixture over shells. Top with remaining mozzarella cheese and sprinkle with parsley.

Cover and bake for 30 minutes; uncover and continue to bake for an additional 10 minutes or until cheese is lightly browned.

LAYERED EGGPLANT AND ZUCCHINI BAKE

This is my version of vegetarian lasagne. I use eggplant instead of noodles in this Italian classic.

PREPARATION TIME:

25 minutes

COOKING TIME:

55 – 60 minutes

SERVINGS: **8**

1   14½-ounce can diced tomatoes, drained
1   15-ounce can tomato sauce
1   6-ounce can tomato paste
1   small onion, finely chopped
2   teaspoons minced garlic
1   tablespoon dried basil leaves
2   large eggplant, cut into ¼-inch slices
2   medium zucchini, cut into ½-inch slices
2   large green bell peppers, thinly sliced
1   4-ounce can sliced black olives
1   cup (4-ounce package) shredded reduced-fat mozzarella cheese
½   cup grated Parmesan cheese

Preheat oven to 350 degrees.

In a medium saucepan, combine diced tomatoes, tomato sauce, tomato paste, onion, garlic, and basil; stir well. Cook over medium heat until bubbling.

In a 13 x 9-inch baking dish, layer ⅓ eggplant, zucchini, bell peppers, and black olives; sprinkle ⅓ of the mozzarella cheese and ⅓ of the tomato sauce over first layer. Repeat for second and third layers until all ingredients are used. Sprinkle Parmesan cheese over top.

Cover and bake for 45 minutes; uncover and continue to bake for an additional 10-15 minutes. Let lasagne set for 10 minutes before serving.

PER SERVING:
Calories: 203
% Calories from Fat: 37
Fat (gm): 9.3
Saturated Fat (gm): 1.9
Cholesterol (mg): 9.9
Sodium (mg): 1228
Protein (gm): 10.8
Carbohydrates (gm): 24.3

EXCHANGES:
Milk: 0.0
Vegetable: 4.0
Fruit: 0.0
Bread: 0.0
Meat: 1.0
Fat: 1.0

VEAL SCALLOPINI

*Fettuccine or linguine noodles are a good accompaniment to this dish. I rec-
ommend preparing them separately so they will be firm and fresh. You can
place the pasta in the bottom of the casserole uncooked, but it tends to get
soft and sticky. No additional cooking time is necessary for this procedure.*

PREPARATION TIME:

20 minutes

COOKING TIME:

1 1/2 hours

SERVINGS: **6 – 8**

1	tablespoon margarine
1 1/2–2	pounds veal, sliced thin and cut into 2-inch strips, uncooked
1/2	cup flour, in zip-style bag
1	16-ounce package mushrooms, rinsed and sliced
1	teaspoon minced garlic
1	tablespoon dried parsley flakes
1	tablespoon dried basil leaves
3/4	cup sherry, *or* red wine
1	8-ounce package fettuccine, *or* linguine, noodles

Preheat oven to 325 degrees.

In a 2 1/2-quart casserole, spread margarine.

Coat strips of veal with flour by putting a few strips at a time in zip-style bag and
shaking. Place veal in casserole.

Spread mushrooms over meat and sprinkle garlic, parsley, and basil evenly over mushrooms; pour wine over entire dish.

Cover and bake for 1 1/2 hours. Serve over noodles.

PER SERVING:
Calories: 394
% Calories from Fat: 21
Fat (gm): 9.3
Saturated Fat (gm): 2
Cholesterol (mg): 99.5
Sodium (mg): 166
Protein (gm): 34.9
Carbohydrates (gm): 35.6

EXCHANGES:
Milk: 0.0
Vegetable: 1.0
Fruit: 0.0
Bread: 2.0
Meat: 4.0
Fat: 0.0

STIR-FRY FISH AND VEGETABLE BAKE

My husband goes on two big fishing trips each year and comes home with a large variety of fresh fish. I have tried to come up with unique ideas for cooking them, other than the traditional "Friday Night Fish Fry." This is one of our favorites that combines the rough textures of stir-fry vegetables with the smoothness of the fish. Have your fishmonger skin the fish.

PREPARATION TIME:

15 minutes

COOKING TIME:

40 – 45 minutes

SERVINGS: **6**

1	teaspoon dried basil
1	teaspoon dried parsley
1	teaspoon dried mustard
1	teaspoon garlic powder
1/4	teaspoon white pepper
1/4	teaspoon cayenne pepper
2	walleye, *or* trout, fillets (about 1 pound each), *or* similar white fish, skin removed
1	16-ounce package frozen stir-fry vegetables, cooked and well drained
4	green onion stalks, finely chopped, including some stems
1/4	cup light soy sauce

Preheat oven to 325 degrees.

In a small bowl, combine basil, parsley, mustard, garlic, white and cayenne pepper. Sprinkle seasonings evenly over one side of each fillet.

In a 13 x 9-inch baking dish, place 1 fillet seasoned side up. Top with vegetables and onions; sprinkle with soy sauce. Place remaining fillet, seasoned side up, on vegetables.

Cover tightly and bake for 40-45 minutes. Fish should be firm, opaque, and just beginning to flake.

PER SERVING:
Calories: 181.8
% Calories from Fat: 11
Fat (gm): 2.2
Saturated Fat (gm): 0.4
Cholesterol (mg): 133.6
Sodium (mg): 446.8
Protein (gm): 31.7
Carbohydrates (gm): 6.8

EXCHANGES:
Milk: 0.0
Vegetable: 0.0
Fruit: 0.0
Bread: 0.0
Meat: 4.0
Fat: 0.0

CHICKEN STUFFED WITH VEGETABLES

The stuffing makes this dish very colorful as well as flavorful.

PREPARATION TIME:

20 minutes

COOKING TIME:

40 minutes

SERVINGS: **6**

PER SERVING:

Calories: 406
% Calories from Fat: 11
Fat (gm): 5.1
Saturated Fat (gm): 1.3
Cholesterol (mg): 73.2
Sodium (mg): 140
Protein (gm): 34
Carbohydrates (gm): 54.9

EXCHANGES:

Milk: 0.0
Vegetable: 0.0
Fruit: 0.0
Bread: 3.5
Meat: 3.0
Fat: 0.0

Vegetable cooking spray
2 cups brown rice, cooked *al dente*
6 boneless, skinless chicken breast halves
1 8-ounce package mushrooms, sliced
1 large carrot, finely chopped
2 green onion stalks, coarsely chopped
1 celery stalk, finely chopped
1 large tomato, peeled, seeded, and chopped
$\frac{1}{2}$ teaspoon dried thyme, divided
$\frac{1}{8}$ teaspoon black pepper, freshly ground, if possible
1 cup low-sodium, fat-free chicken broth
$\frac{1}{4}$ cup skim milk
$1\frac{1}{2}$ tablespoons flour

Preheat oven to 350 degrees.

Lightly coat a 13 x 9-inch baking dish with cooking spray.

Spread rice evenly in bottom of dish. Set aside.

Place each chicken breast between waxed paper. Using a mallet or a large wooden spoon, pound to about $\frac{1}{4}$ inch thickness. Remove paper.

In a medium bowl, combine mushrooms, carrot, onion, celery, tomato, half of the thyme, and pepper. Mix together well. Spoon equal amounts of the vegetable mixture onto the center of each chicken breast. Fold in sides and roll up jelly-roll style; secure with wooden toothpicks and place over rice in baking dish.

In a small saucepan, combine broth, milk, and flour stirring until flour is dissolved. Over low heat, continue to stir until sauce starts to thicken. Pour over chicken. Sprinkle remaining thyme over sauce.

Cover and bake for 40 minutes.

PORK MEDALLIONS WITH SPINACH PASTA AND YOGURT SAUCE

This delicious casserole sounds harder to prepare than it actually is. The combination of apples and yogurt make a sauce that is light and refreshing.

PREPARATION TIME:

20 minutes

COOKING TIME:

I hour

SERVINGS: **4**

I 8-ounce package spinach pasta (fettuccine, linguine, or other pasta), cooked for 3 minutes

¾ pound pork tenderloin, trimmed and cut into ½-inch slices (have it cut by the butcher)

2 medium apples, cut into ½-inch slices

½ cup unsweetened apple juice

I small onion, finely chopped

⅛ teaspoon salt

¼ teaspoon dried crushed sage

2 tablespoons flour

I 8-ounce container plain low-fat yogurt

I tablespoon chives, coarsely chopped

4 tiny red onions, halved

Preheat oven to 325 degrees.

In a 2½-quart casserole, evenly space pasta.

Place pork medallions on top of pasta, overlapping if necessary, and place apples on top of meat.

In a small skillet, combine apple juice, chopped onion, salt, and sage. Cover and cook over medium heat until onion is tender, about 5 minutes. Stir flour into yogurt and slowly add to skillet, continuing to stir over medium heat until thickened.

Spoon sauce over casserole and top with chives and red onions.

Cover and bake for I hour or until bubbly.

PER SERVING:
Calories: 390
% Calories from Fat: 16
Fat (gm): 6.9
Saturated Fat (gm): 2.3
Cholesterol (mg): 106
Sodium (mg): 190
Protein (gm): 29.4
Carbohydrates (gm): 53.4

EXCHANGES:
Milk: 0.0
Vegetable: 0.0
Fruit: 1.0
Bread: 2.0
Meat: 3.0
Fat: 0.0

SHISH-KABOB CASSEROLE

Chicken, beef, shrimp, or—for something a little different—scallops can be used in this easy-to-create casserole. I used skinless chicken breasts for this dish. When using shrimp or scallops, reduce baking time by 10 minutes.

PREPARATION TIME:

15 minutes

COOKING TIME:

35 minutes

SERVINGS: 4

1 large green bell pepper, seeded and cut into 1½-inch pieces
1 large red bell pepper, seeded and cut into 1½-inch pieces
1 large white onion, cut into eighths
8 8-inch wooden skewers, *or* 4, 12-inch metal skewers
1 pound meat, *or* seafood, cut into 1-inch pieces
1 pint cherry tomatoes
1 8-ounce package mushrooms, whole
2 tablespoons margarine
2 tablespoons dried tarragon
½ cup flour
2 tablespoons Dijon mustard
1 cup dry white wine, *or* 2 tablespoons white wine vinegar
and ¾ cup water

PER SERVING:
Calories: 373
% Calories from Fat: 24
Fat (gm): 10.3
Saturated Fat (gm): 2.1
Cholesterol (mg): 69
Sodium (mg): 245
Protein (gm): 31.6
Carbohydrates (gm): 30.9

EXCHANGES:
Milk: 0.0
Vegetable: 3.0
Fruit: 0.0
Bread: 1.0
Meat: 3.0
Fat: 1.0

Preheat oven to 350 degrees.

In a medium microwave-safe bowl, combine peppers and onion (try not to separate onion pieces). Place a damp paper towel over vegetables and microwave on high for 2½ minutes.

On each skewer, alternate pepper, onion, meat, tomato, mushroom, and another pepper until skewer is full. Try to start and end with a pepper, as they stay on the skewer best.

Place shish-kabobs in a 13 x 9-inch baking dish, overlapping if necessary. Set aside.

In a small saucepan, melt margarine over medium heat. Add tarragon and flour. Gradually add mustard and white wine; continue to heat for 2-3 minutes until thickened. Pour over shish-kabobs.

Cover and bake for 35 minutes.

ASPARAGUS-ROUGHY AU GRATIN

Orange roughy is meaty and light tasting—not too fishy.

  2 cups minute, *or* boil-in-bag, rice, cooked according to package directions
  1 pound fresh asparagus spears, cut into 1-inch pieces
  6 6-ounce orange roughy fillets
  3 tablespoons margarine
  1 medium onion, finely chopped
$\frac{1}{3}$ cup flour
  1 cup skim milk
  1 cup shredded reduced-fat Cheddar cheese
$\frac{1}{4}$ teaspoon salt
$\frac{1}{4}$ teaspoon black pepper, freshly ground, if possible
  1 cup unseasoned breadcrumbs

Preheat oven to 350 degrees.

Spread rice and asparagus evenly over bottom of 13 x 9-inch baking dish. Arrange fillets, slightly overlapping, on top of asparagus. Set aside.

In a small saucepan, melt margarine over medium heat. Add onion; cook for 3 to 5 minutes. Stir in flour; gradually add milk. Heat for an additional 3-5 minutes until mixture thickens, stirring continuously. Stir in cheese, salt, and pepper.

Spoon sauce evenly over fish fillets. Sprinkle breadcrumbs evenly over sauce.

Cover and bake for 35 minutes or until sauce is bubbly; uncover and bake for an additional 10 minutes to brown top. Let stand for 10 minutes before serving.

PREPARATION TIME:
20 minutes
COOKING TIME:
45 minutes
SERVINGS: **6**

PER SERVING:
Calories: 470
% Calories from Fat: 21
Fat (gm): 11
Saturated Fat (gm): 2.9
Cholesterol (mg): 44.2
Sodium (mg): 703
Protein (gm): 37.3
Carbohydrates (gm): 53.5

EXCHANGES:
Milk: 0.0
Vegetable: 1.0
Fruit: 0.0
Bread: 3.0
Meat: 3.0
Fat: 1.0

SALMON, PEA POD, AND NEW POTATO CASSEROLE

Using lemon gives this casserole a light, delicate flavor.

PREPARATION TIME:
15 minutes

COOKING TIME:
35 – 40 minutes

SERVINGS: *4*

Vegetable cooking spray
4 salmon fillets, approximately 6 ounces each
2 tablespoons margarine, softened
1 tablespoon dried tarragon
1 small lemon, thinly sliced
1 8-ounce package frozen pea pods, thawed and drained
12 baby new potatoes, halved
$\frac{1}{2}$ tablespoon black pepper, freshly ground, if possible
$\frac{1}{3}$ cup apple cider

Preheat oven to 325 degrees.

Lightly coat a 13 x 9-inch baking dish with cooking spray. Place salmon fillets in dish and spread each fillet with $\frac{1}{2}$ tablespoon of softened margarine. Sprinkle fillets with tarragon and cover with lemon slices.

Place pea pods and potatoes randomly around fillets, wherever there is space; sprinkle with black pepper. Pour cider over entire dish.

Cover and bake for 35-40 minutes or until fillets flake and potatoes are soft.

PER SERVING:
Calories: 593
% Calories from Fat: 15
Fat (gm): 10.1
Saturated Fat (gm): 1.8
Cholesterol (mg): 57.5
Sodium (mg): 171
Protein (gm): 32.1
Carbohydrates (gm): 96.8

EXCHANGES:
Milk: 0.0
Vegetable: 0.0
Fruit: 0.0
Bread: 6.0
Meat: 3.0
Fat: 0.0

PORK TENDERLOIN WITH APRICOT STUFFING

This is an elegant dish that is much easier to prepare than the name suggests.

  1 pound pork tenderloin, split lengthwise, cutting to, but not through, opposite side
  1 instant chicken, *or* vegetable, bouillon cube
  1 8½-ounce can apricots, drained, reserving liquid
  1 stalk celery, finely chopped
  1 small onion, finely chopped
  ⅛ teaspoon ground cinnamon
  ⅛ teaspoon black pepper, freshly ground, if possible
  2 cups seasoned bread cubes
  2 cups minute, *or* boil-in-bag, rice, cooked according to package directions
  1½ teaspoons cornstarch
  ⅛ teaspoon ground nutmeg

Preheat oven to 325 degrees.

Spread tenderloin flat and pound lightly with meat mallet to approximately a 10 x 6-inch rectangle.

In a medium saucepan over low heat, dissolve bouillon in ⅔ cup hot water. Remove from heat; add apricots and let stand 5 minutes. Stir in celery, onion, cinnamon, pepper, and bread cubes.

Spread stuffing mixture evenly over tenderloin. Roll up jelly-roll style, starting from short side. Secure meat roll with wooden toothpicks or tie with string at 1-inch intervals. Cut meat roll into six 1-inch slices.

Evenly spread rice in bottom of 12 x 8-inch glass baking dish. Place meat slices over rice, cut sides down.

In a small saucepan, combine reserved apricot juice, cornstarch, and nutmeg. Stir over low heat until mixture thickens, about 3 minutes. Pour over meat and rice.

Cover and bake for 50 minutes.

PREPARATION TIME:
20 minutes
COOKING TIME:
50 minutes
SERVINGS: 6

PER SERVING:
Calories: 278
% Calories from Fat: 10
Fat (gm): 3.2
Saturated Fat (gm): 1
Cholesterol (mg): 43.6
Sodium (mg): 446
Protein (gm): 20
Carbohydrates (gm): 41.2

EXCHANGES:
Milk: 0.0
Vegetable: 0.0
Fruit: 0.5
Bread: 2.0
Meat: 2.0
Fat: 0.0

SALMON SOUFFLÉ

This casserole takes a little care in preparation, but the results are worth every minute.

PREPARATION TIME:
20 minutes
COOKING TIME:
45 – 50 minutes
SERVINGS: *6*

Vegetable cooking spray
1 small green bell pepper, coarsely chopped
1 small red bell pepper, coarsely chopped
1 10-ounce package frozen corn
2 tablespoons margarine
$1/4$ cup flour
$3/4$ teaspoon dried dill weed
$1/4$ teaspoon salt
$1/8$ teaspoon white pepper
$1\frac{1}{2}$ cups skim milk
4 egg yolks, lightly beaten
1 $6\frac{1}{2}$-ounce can boneless, skinless salmon, drained
5 egg whites
Pinch cream of tartar

Preheat oven to 350 degrees.

Coat a 2-quart soufflé dish with cooking spray. Set aside.

In a medium mixing bowl, combine green and red peppers, corn, and margarine. Cover with plastic wrap; microwave, on high, for 4-6 minutes or until vegetables are tender. Stir in flour, dill weed, salt, and pepper. Gradually blend in milk.

Microwave, on high, uncovered, for 7-8 minutes or until mixture thickens and bubbles, stirring every 2 minutes. Gradually stir a small amount of hot vegetable mixture into egg yolks; blend yolks back into bowl of vegetable mixture. Add salmon and mix well. Set aside.

In a large mixing bowl, using an electric mixer, beat egg whites until frothy; add cream of tartar, and continue beating until stiff but not dry. Fold into salmon-vegetable mixture. Pour all into coated soufflé dish.

Bake, uncovered, for 45 to 50 minutes or until golden brown and knife inserted in center comes out clean.

PER SERVING:
Calories: 223
% Calories from Fat: 38
Fat (gm): 9.7
Saturated Fat (gm): 2.4
Cholesterol (mg): 156.4
Sodium (mg): 383
Protein (gm): 15.6
Carbohydrates (gm): 19.5

EXCHANGES:
Milk: 0.0
Vegetable: 0.0
Fruit: 0.0
Bread: 1.0
Meat: 2.0
Fat: 1.0

oodles of noodles

Veal and Peppers Pasta

Spinach Tortellini with Mushrooms

Chicken and Noodles

Baked Rigatoni

Noodle Kugel

Eggplant Parmigiana

Caper Chicken with Tomato-Basil Linguine

Mushroom-Zucchini Lasagne

Turkey Bow Tie Pasta au Gratin

Garlic Chicken and Tri-Colored Pasta

Spicy Tomato Vegetable Linguine

Beef Stroganoff

Seafood Newburg

Spicy Beef and Asparagus with Rice Noodles

VEAL AND PEPPERS PASTA

The red sweet pepper and lima beans brighten up this tasty casserole.

- 1 8-ounce package pepper linguine, cooked *al dente*
- 1 pound veal cutlets, thinly sliced into strips
- 1 red bell pepper, seeded and thinly sliced
- 1 8-ounce package mushrooms, halved
- 1 15-ounce can lima beans, drained
- 1 tablespoon margarine
- 2 tablespoons flour
- ¾ cup skim milk
- 1 tablespoon capers

Preheat oven to 350 degrees.

Evenly spread pasta in the bottom of a 10 x 10-inch baking dish.

Place veal strips over the pasta, overlapping if necessary.

In a medium bowl, combine bell pepper, mushrooms, and lima beans. Spoon over the veal.

In a small saucepan, over medium heat, melt margarine. Mix in flour; gradually stir in milk and add capers. Pour sauce over veal and vegetables.

Cover and bake for 40 minutes.

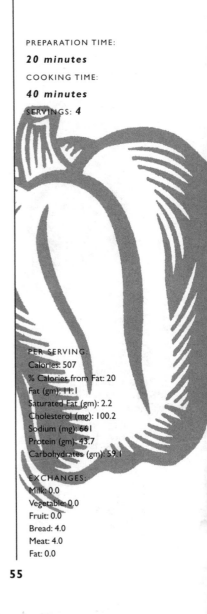

PREPARATION TIME:
20 minutes
COOKING TIME:
40 minutes
SERVINGS: **4**

PER SERVING:
Calories: 507
% Calories from Fat: 20
Fat (gm): 11.1
Saturated Fat (gm): 2.2
Cholesterol (mg): 100.2
Sodium (mg): 661
Protein (gm): 43.7
Carbohydrates (gm): 59.1

EXCHANGES:
Milk: 0.0
Vegetable: 0.0
Fruit: 0.0
Bread: 4.0
Meat: 4.0
Fat: 0.0

SPINACH TORTELLINI WITH MUSHROOMS

This hearty casserole is a snap to make, using mostly prepared ingredients.

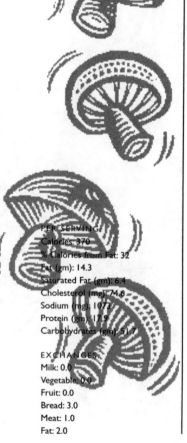

1 16-ounce package frozen spinach tortellini, thawed

1 16-ounce package mushrooms, whole

1 medium red bell pepper, coarsely chopped

1 cup (4-ounce package) shredded reduced-fat mozzarella cheese

1 28-ounce jar spaghetti sauce, any flavor

Preheat oven to 350 degrees.

In a 2½-quart casserole, combine tortellini, mushrooms, bell pepper, and cheese.

Pour sauce evenly over casserole.

Cover and bake for 40 minutes.

PREPARATION TIME:
10 minutes

COOKING TIME:
40 minutes

SERVINGS: 6

PER SERVING:
Calories: 370
% Calories from Fat: 32
Fat (gm): 14.3
Saturated Fat (gm): 6.4
Cholesterol (mg): 74.6
Sodium (mg): 1073
Protein (gm): 17.9
Carbohydrates (gm): 51.7

EXCHANGES:
Milk: 0.0
Vegetable: 0.0
Fruit: 0.0
Bread: 3.0
Meat: 1.0
Fat: 2.0

CHICKEN AND NOODLES

This is another "comfort" casserole from my childhood. My mother used Kluski noodles, a narrow noodle with more substance than regular egg noodles. I have a hard time finding the Kluski noodles now, so I usually use thin egg noodles and still get the same satisfaction I did when my mom made this dish for us.

PREPARATION TIME:

15 minutes

COOKING TIME:

30 minutes

SERVINGS: **4**

- 3 tablespoons margarine
- $\frac{1}{3}$ cup flour
- $\frac{1}{4}$ teaspoon dried, crushed sage
- $\frac{1}{4}$ teaspoon dried marjoram
- 1 13$\frac{3}{4}$-ounce can low-sodium, fat-free chicken broth
- $\frac{1}{4}$ cup skim milk
- $\frac{1}{4}$ teaspoon black pepper, freshly ground, if possible
- 3 tablespoons diced pimientos
- 1 10-ounce package frozen mixed vegetables, thawed and drained
- 4 boneless, skinless chicken breast halves, cut into 1-inch pieces
- 1 8-ounce package thin noodles, cooked *al dente*
- $\frac{1}{2}$ cup unseasoned breadcrumbs

Preheat oven to 350 degrees.

Melt margarine in large saucepan over medium heat and blend in flour, sage, and marjoram. Gradually stir in broth and milk; add pepper and pimientos while continuing to stir. Heat until mixture thickens, 3-4 minutes. Remove from heat.

In a 2-quart casserole, combine vegetables, chicken, and noodles. Pour sauce over top to cover evenly. Sprinkle breadcrumbs over top.

Bake, uncovered, for 30 minutes or until browned and bubbly.

PER SERVING:
Calories: 599
% Calories from Fat: 23
Fat (gm): 16
Saturated Fat (gm): 3.2
Cholesterol (mg): 127
Sodium (mg): 355
Protein (gm): 41.6
Carbohydrates (gm): 69.5

EXCHANGES:
Milk: 0.0
Vegetable: 2.0
Fruit: 0.0
Bread: 4.0
Meat: 3.0
Fat: 2.0

BAKED RIGATONI

My husband, Craig, created this quick and easy casserole.

PREPARATION TIME:
15 minutes
COOKING TIME:
40 minutes
SERVINGS: *6*

1 16-ounce package rigatoni noodles, cooked *al dente*
1 10-ounce package frozen spinach, thawed and well drained
1 8-ounce package mushrooms, coarsely chopped
1 28-ounce jar spaghetti sauce, any flavor
1 cup (4-ounce package) shredded reduced-fat mozzarella cheese
1 large tomato, thinly sliced

Preheat oven to 350 degrees.

In a 13 x 9-inch baking dish, combine rigatoni, spinach, and mushrooms.

Pour sauce evenly over noodles and vegetables. Sprinkle cheese over sauce and place tomato slices on top of cheese, overlapping if necessary.

Cover and bake for 30 minutes; uncover and continue to bake for an additional 10 minutes.

PER SERVING:
Calories: 519
% Calories from Fat: 18
Fat (gm): 10.2
Saturated Fat (gm): 4.1
Cholesterol (mg): 34.6
Sodium (mg): 903
Protein (gm): 19.5
Carbohydrates (gm): 86.8

EXCHANGES:
Milk: 0.0
Vegetable: 0.0
Fruit: 0.0
Bread: 6.0
Meat: 0.0
Fat: 2.0

NOODLE KUGEL

This old-fashioned, pot-luck dish is a great cold weather meal—it is quick and easy to fix and hearty, yet not too heavy. You can substitute no-yolk noodles for egg noodles, keeping the same flavor, but the noodles won't stay quite as firm. This casserole can be prepared ahead of time and refrigerated. Remove from refrigerator 20 minutes before baking. There is no need to increase baking time.

PREPARATION TIME:
15 minutes
COOKING TIME:
45 minutes
SERVINGS: **6**

1	8-ounce package thin egg noodles, uncooked
1½	pounds lean ground beef
1	large onion, finely chopped
1	large green bell pepper, coarsely chopped
1	10-ounce package frozen corn, uncooked
1	14½-ounce can diced tomatoes, undrained
½	teaspoon black pepper, freshly ground, if possible
1	cup seasoned breadcrumbs

Preheat oven to 350 degrees.

In a medium pot, bring 4 cups of water to a boil; stir in noodles and bring to boil, cooking for 4-6 minutes (noodles will not be thoroughly cooked). Remove from heat, drain, and set aside.

Brown beef and onion in a medium skillet. Remove from heat and drain any excess liquid. Add peppers, corn, tomatoes, and black pepper; mix well.

Combine the noodles with beef mixture in a 2–2½-quart casserole; sprinkle bread-crumbs over top.

Bake, uncovered, for 45 minutes.

PER SERVING:
Calories: 503
% Calories from Fat: 31
Fat (gm): 17.2
Saturated Fat (gm): 6.4
Cholesterol (mg): 106
Sodium (mg): 719
Protein (gm): 30.6
Carbohydrates (gm): 56.8

EXCHANGES:
Milk: 0.0
Vegetable: 2.0
Fruit: 0.0
Bread: 3.0
Meat: 3.0
Fat: 1.5

EGGPLANT PARMIGIANA

A wonderful meatless dish that has all the flavor of the Italian favorite but is simple to prepare. Serve with linguine. This is an excellent casserole to prepare ahead of time and refrigerate for future use—no need to increase cooking time.

PREPARATION TIME:

25 minutes

COOKING TIME:

1¼ hours

SERVINGS: *4 – 6*

Vegetable cooking spray
3 large eggplants, cut into ¼-inch slices
2 eggs, lightly beaten
2 tablespoons skim milk
2 cups unseasoned breadcrumbs
½ cup grated Parmesan cheese
Large zip-style bag
2 14½-ounce cans diced tomatoes, undrained
1 6-ounce can tomato paste
½ small onion, finely chopped
1 small green bell pepper, thinly sliced
2 teaspoons dried basil
1½ teaspoons dried oregano
1 teaspoon minced garlic
1 large zucchini, cut into thin slices
2 cups (8-ounce package) shredded reduced-fat mozzarella cheese, divided
1 8-ounce package linguine, cooked

Preheat oven to 350 degrees.

Coat a 13 x 9-inch glass baking dish with cooking spray, or use a non-stick metal pan. Soak eggplant in water while preparing other ingredients.

In a small bowl, mix beaten eggs and skim milk. In a large zip-style bag, mix breadcrumbs and Parmesan cheese. Set aside.

In a medium bowl, combine tomatoes, tomato paste, onion, bell pepper, basil, oregano, and garlic; mix well. Set aside.

Drain eggplant slices and place on paper towels. Take one slice and dip it into egg mixture, coating entire slice. Then put coated slice into plastic bag and shake. Repeat until all slices are breaded.

Place 1 layer of breaded eggplant on bottom of baking dish (overlapping), 1 layer of zucchini on top, followed by $\frac{1}{3}$ cup of mozzarella cheese. Pour $\frac{1}{3}$ of tomato mixture over cheese. Repeat layers twice.

Cover and bake for 1 hour; uncover and bake for an additional 15 minutes. Let casserole set for 10 minutes before serving. Serve over linguine.

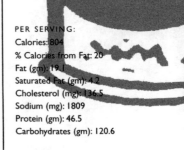

PER SERVING:
Calories: 804
% Calories from Fat: 20
Fat (gm): 19.1
Saturated Fat (gm): 4.2
Cholesterol (mg): 136.5
Sodium (mg): 1809
Protein (gm): 46.5
Carbohydrates (gm): 120.6

EXCHANGES:
Milk: 0.0
Vegetable: 3.0
Fruit: 0.0
Bread: 6.5
Meat: 4.0
Fat: 1.0

CAPER CHICKEN WITH TOMATO-BASIL LINGUINE

The lemon and capers add a flavor that nicely complements the textures of this light dish that is quick and easy to prepare.

PREPARATION TIME:

15 minutes

COOKING TIME:

40 minutes

SERVINGS: *4*

1	13¾-ounce can low-sodium, fat-free chicken broth
2	tablespoons arrowroot (a thickener similar to cornstarch)
3	tablespoons lemon juice
2½	tablespoons diced pimientos
2	tablespoons capers with juice
1	8-ounce package fresh mushrooms, rinsed and sliced
1	10-ounce package frozen broccoli pieces
1	8-ounce can sliced water chestnuts
1	8-ounce package basil-tomato, *or* plain, linguine, uncooked
4	boneless, skinless chicken breast halves, cut into 1-inch strips

Preheat oven to 350 degrees.

In a small sauce pan, combine chicken broth and arrowroot. Over low heat, stir occasionally until thickened. (Broth will remain clear; if using cornstarch, broth will turn white color.) Remove from heat immediately. Stir in lemon juice, pimientos, and capers. Set aside.

In a large bowl, combine mushrooms, broccoli, and water chestnuts; mix well.

Spread uncooked linguine over bottom of 9 x 13-inch non-stick baking dish, or use a lightly greased glass dish.

Place chicken strips on top of pasta, then spread vegetables over chicken. Pour sauce over other ingredients to coat evenly.

Cover tightly and bake, on center rack of oven, for 40 minutes.

PER SERVING:

Calories: 314
% Calories from Fat: 13
Fat (gm): 4.8
Saturated Fat (gm): 0.9
Cholesterol (mg): 73
Sodium (mg): 318
Protein (gm): 35.1
Carbohydrates (gm): 33.8

EXCHANGES:

Milk: 0.0
Vegetable: 2.0
Fruit: 0.0
Bread: 1.5
Meat: 3.0
Fat: 0.0

MUSHROOM-ZUCCHINI LASAGNE

This vegetable lasagne has a béchamel (white) sauce instead of the standard tomato-based sauce.

2 tablespoons margarine
3 tablespoons flour
2 cups skim milk
1 bay leaf
1 tablespoon dried basil
1 tablespoon dried parsley
1 tablespoon dried marjoram
2 tablespoons grated Parmesan cheese
1 15-ounce package lasagne noodles, cooked *al dente*
1 15-ounce container fat-free ricotta cheese
1 16-ounce package mushrooms, thickly sliced
3 medium zucchini, thickly sliced
1 large tomato, thinly sliced

Preheat oven to 350 degrees.

In a medium saucepan over medium heat, melt the margarine and reduce heat. Add flour, stirring continuously until blended; this smooth mixture is called a roux. Add milk gradually, blending well so that the sauce is smooth. Mix in bay leaf, basil, parsley, marjoram, and Parmesan cheese. Keep over low heat, stirring occasionally, while preparing rest of casserole.

In a 13 x 9-inch baking dish, place 3 lasagne noodles lengthwise; break a noodle in half to fill entire dish length. Spread 1/3 of ricotta over noodles. Place a layer of mushrooms and zucchini over ricotta. Using a large ladle, spoon 1/4 of white sauce over vegetables. Repeat layers two more times, alternating the pattern of noodles. Top the last cheese/vegetable layer with noodles (there may be a few noodles left over) and remaining white sauce; then place tomato slices on top.

Cover and bake for 40 minutes; uncover and continue to bake for an additional 10 minutes.

PREPARATION TIME:
20 minutes
COOKING TIME:
50 minutes
SERVINGS: **6**

PER SERVING:
Calories: 336
% Calories from Fat: 20
Fat (gm): 7.8
Saturated Fat (gm): 1.3
Cholesterol (mg): 3
Sodium (mg): 187
Protein (gm): 22.9
Carbohydrates (gm): 48.9

EXCHANGES:
Milk: 0.0
Vegetable: 0.0
Fruit: 0.0
Bread: 3.0
Meat: 2.0
Fat: 0.0

63

TURKEY BOW-TIE PASTA AU GRATIN

This casserole originated as a cold salad. In colder weather I wanted that same flavor in a hot version, so I created this dish.

PREPARATION TIME:
15 minutes

COOKING TIME:
45 minutes

SERVINGS: **6**

1   16-ounce package bow-tie pasta, cooked *al dente*
1   pound skinless turkey breast, or strips, cooked and cut into 1-inch pieces
1   10-ounce package frozen broccoli pieces, thawed and well drained
1   celery stalk, finely chopped
$\frac{1}{2}$ cup low-sodium, fat-free chicken broth
$\frac{1}{2}$ cup fat-free sour cream
1   tablespoon dried dill weed
1   teaspoon black pepper, freshly ground, if possible
1   cup (4-ounce package) shredded reduced-fat mozzarella cheese
$\frac{1}{2}$ cup unseasoned breadcrumbs

Preheat oven to 350 degrees.

In a 2–2$\frac{1}{2}$-quart casserole, combine pasta, turkey, broccoli, and celery. Set aside.

Mix broth, sour cream, dill, and pepper in a medium bowl until blended. Stir into pasta mixture.

Sprinkle cheese over the pasta and top with breadcrumbs.

Cover and bake for 30 minutes; uncover and bake an additional 15 minutes.

Note: A quick method of cooking turkey breast strips is to put the meat in a shallow microwavable dish and microwave for 2 minutes on high. Stir meat, turn dish, and cook on high for 3 additional minutes. Add another minute if you feel turkey isn't quite cooked through—microwave cooking times do vary.

PER SERVING:
Calories: 512
% Calories from Fat: 9
Fat (gm): 5.2
Saturated Fat (gm): 2.5
Cholesterol (mg): 73.1
Sodium (mg): 312
Protein (gm): 42.4
Carbohydrates (gm): 71.1

EXCHANGES:
Milk: 0.0
Vegetable: 2.0
Fruit: 0.0
Bread: 4.0
Meat: 4.0
Fat: 0.0

GARLIC CHICKEN AND TRI-COLORED PASTA

Any combination of vegetables will enhance this brightly colored casserole.

1   16-ounce package tri-colored pasta (rotini, mostaccioli, or rigatoni)
6   boneless, skinless chicken breast halves
1   10-ounce package frozen mixed vegetables, thawed and well drained
2   tablespoons flour
$\frac{1}{2}$ cup skim milk
1   13$\frac{3}{4}$-ounce can low-sodium, fat-free chicken broth
1   teaspoon black pepper, freshly ground, if possible
2   teaspoons minced garlic
1   teaspoon dried rosemary

Preheat oven to 350 degrees.

Place uncooked pasta in a 2$\frac{1}{2}$-quart casserole. Arrange chicken breasts on top of pasta. Spread vegetables over chicken.

In a small bowl, mix together flour and milk. Slowly add broth, then stir in pepper, garlic, and rosemary. Pour over pasta, chicken, and vegetables.

Cover and bake for 55 minutes.

PREPARATION TIME:
15 minutes
COOKING TIME:
55 minutes
SERVINGS: 6

PER SERVING:
Calories: 486
% Calories from Fat: 9
Fat (gm): 4.6
Saturated Fat (gm): 1.1
Cholesterol (mg): 73.3
Sodium (mg): 196
Protein (gm): 40.4
Carbohydrates (gm): 68.5

EXCHANGES:
Milk: 0.0
Vegetable: 1.0
Fruit: 0.0
Bread: 4.0
Meat: 3.0
Fat: 0.0

SPICY TOMATO-VEGETABLE LINGUINE

My husband's love of peppers inspired me to create this slightly spicy casserole.

PREPARATION TIME:

20 minutes

COOKING TIME:

40 minutes

SERVINGS: **4**

1 green bell pepper, coarsely chopped

2 banana peppers, finely chopped

1 medium yellow onion, finely chopped

1 $14\frac{1}{2}$-ounce can diced tomatoes, with liquid

2 yellow squash, thickly sliced

2 zucchini, thickly sliced

1 8-ounce can tomato sauce

1 6-ounce can tomato paste

2 teaspoons minced garlic

$\frac{1}{4}$ teaspoon cayenne pepper

1 8-ounce package linguine, cooked *al dente*

Preheat oven to 350 degrees.

In a large bowl, combine bell pepper, banana pepper, onion, tomatoes, all but 6 slices of squash, zucchini, tomato sauce, tomato paste, garlic, and cayenne pepper. Mix well.

Place linguine in a 2-quart casserole. Spoon vegetable mixture over pasta. Top with reserved squash slices.

Cover and bake for 40 minutes.

PER SERVING:
Calories: 304
% Calories from Fat: 9
Fat (gm): 3.3
Saturated Fat (gm): 0.2
Cholesterol (mg): 0
Sodium (mg): 944
Protein (gm): 13.8
Carbohydrates (gm): 61.1

EXCHANGES:
Milk: 0.0
Vegetable: 4.0
Fruit: 0.0
Bread: 2.5
Meat: 0.0
Fat: 0.5

BEEF STROGANOFF

When preparing this dish ahead of time and refrigerating, reduce cooking time by 15 minutes. The meat will be tender from softening in the stock and the noodles will be very soft. Always add sour cream near the end of baking this casserole to keep the proper consistency and avoid curdling. No-yolk noodles can always be substituted for regular egg noodles to reduce cholesterol.

PREPARATION TIME:

20 minutes

COOKING TIME:

1¼ hours

SERVINGS: 6 — 8

1	12-ounce package wide egg noodles
1½–2	pounds round, *or* sirloin, steak, cut into 1-inch strips
½	cup flour, in zip-style bag
1	16-ounce package mushrooms, rinsed and coarsely chopped
2	tablespoons finely chopped onion
½	teaspoon ground nutmeg
½	teaspoon dried parsley flakes
1	tablespoon paprika
1	13¾-ounce can low-sodium, fat-free beef broth
1	8-ounce container fat-free sour cream

Preheat oven to 325 degrees.

Place uncooked noodles in a 2½-quart casserole.

Coat strips of steak with flour by putting a few strips at a time in zip-style bag and shaking well. Arrange coated meat on top of noodles.

Arrange chopped mushrooms evenly over meat. Then sprinkle the onion, nutmeg, parsley, and paprika on top of mushrooms.

Pour beef broth over entire dish.

Cover and bake for 1 hour; stir in sour cream and bake for an additional 15 minutes.

PER SERVING:
Calories: 385
% Calories from Fat: 16
Fat (gm): 6.9
Saturated Fat (gm): 2.2
Cholesterol (mg): 91.8
Sodium (mg): 100
Protein (gm): 37.5
Carbohydrates (gm): 42.9

EXCHANGES:
Milk: 0.0
Vegetable: 2.0
Fruit: 0.0
Bread: 2.0
Meat: 4.0
Fat: 0.0

SEAFOOD NEWBURG

My version of seafood Newburg calls for fresh asparagus and white wine to give it a subtle flavor. By using margarine and skim milk, this New England favorite is lower in fat. Serve this casserole with fettuccine or linguine, or serve it over toast.

PREPARATION TIME:

15 minutes

COOKING TIME:

35 minutes

SERVINGS: 6

$\frac{1}{2}$ pound bay scallops

$\frac{1}{2}$ pound medium shrimp, shelled and deveined

$\frac{1}{2}$ pound crab meat

1 pound fresh asparagus

1 10-ounce package frozen corn, thawed and drained

3 tablespoons margarine

$\frac{1}{4}$ cup flour

2 cups skim milk

$\frac{1}{4}$ teaspoon black pepper, freshly ground, if possible

$\frac{1}{4}$ cup dry white wine

Preheat oven to 325 degrees.

In a 2$\frac{1}{2}$-quart casserole, combine scallops, shrimp, crab, asparagus, and corn. Set aside.

In a medium saucepan over medium heat, melt the margarine and reduce heat. Add flour, stirring continuously until blended; this smooth mixture is called a roux. Add milk gradually, blending well so that the sauce is smooth. Stir in pepper and wine. If the sauce seems too thin, raise heat a little and cook for a few more minutes to thicken.

Pour the sauce over the seafood and vegetables.

Cover and bake for 35 minutes. Serve over pasta or toast.

PER SERVING:
Calories: 230
% Calories from Fat: 26
Fat (gm): 7
Saturated Fat (gm): 1.4
Cholesterol (mg): 82
Sodium (mg): 281
Protein (gm): 21
Carbohydrates (gm): 21.3

EXCHANGES:
Milk: 0.0
Vegetable: 1.0
Fruit: 0.0
Bread: 1.0
Meat: 2.0
Fat: 0.0

SPICY BEEF AND ASPARAGUS WITH RICE NOODLES

By using frozen stir-fry vegetables, in addition to fresh asparagus, much time is saved in preparing this dish. Adjust the spiciness by reducing the pepper sauce or eliminating it altogether—the flavor will be just as good but not hot. You can also add hot sauce after cooking to suit individual tastes.

1	pound lean top round steak, cut into thin strips
1	8-ounce package rice noodles, soaked in cold water 10 minutes
¾	pound fresh asparagus, cut into 1-inch pieces
1	16-ounce package frozen stir-fry vegetables, thawed and drained
2	tablespoons flour
2	tablespoons water
1	teaspoon dry sherry, *or* red wine (optional)
¼	teaspoon black pepper, freshly ground, if possible
	Hot pepper sauce (you can find small bottles in the ethnic aisle), adjust to taste
1	beef bouillon cube dissolved in ¾ cup hot water
1	tablespoon low-sodium soy sauce
1	tablespoon catsup
1	teaspoon minced garlic

Preheat oven to 350 degrees.

In a 2½-quart casserole, place beef strips, noodles, asparagus, and vegetables.

In a medium bowl, combine flour and water; stir until well blended. Mix in sherry, pepper, pepper sauce, if desired, beef bouillon, soy sauce, catsup, and garlic.

Pour sauce over beef and vegetables.

Cover and bake for 45 minutes.

Note: If fresh vegetables are desired, use 1 small green bell pepper and 1 small red bell pepper, seeded and thinly sliced; 1 small onion, thinly sliced; 1 cup coarsely chopped cauliflower or other desired vegetable, coarsely chopped.

PREPARATION TIME:
20 minutes
COOKING TIME:
45 minutes
SERVINGS: **6**

PER SERVING:
Calories: 289
% Calories from Fat: 11
Fat (gm): 3.6
Saturated Fat (gm): 1.2
Cholesterol (mg): 37.3
Sodium (mg): 326
Protein (gm): 19.8
Carbohydrates (gm): 43.9

EXCHANGES:
Milk: 0.0
Vegetable: 2.0
Fruit: 0.0
Bread: 2.0
Meat: 2.0
Fat: 0.0

great grain
casseroles

Chicken and Rice Roll-Ups

Jambalaya

Wild Rice Casserole

Mushroom Pie

Spicy Chicken and Spanish Rice

Dijon Chicken au Gratin

Polenta and Curried Vegetables

Pollo Mole (Chicken with Brown Sauce)

Beef and Broccoli Teriyaki

Wild Rice with Chicken and Sausage

Barley Mushroom Bake

Sun-Dried Tomato Couscous with Chicken and Mushrooms

CHICKEN AND RICE ROLL-UPS

The colors of the corn, green pepper, and pimientos make this an attractive dish.

2 cups extra-long-grain rice, cooked according to package directions
1 13¾-ounce can low-sodium, fat-free chicken broth
1 cup water
1 10-ounce package frozen corn, cooked and well drained
1 cup finely chopped green bell pepper
3 tablespoons diced pimientos
1 cup shredded Monterey Jack cheese
4 boneless, skinless chicken breast halves
   Black pepper, to taste, freshly ground, if possible

Preheat oven to 325 degrees.

Combine rice and chicken broth in medium saucepan. Bring to a boil; reduce heat, cover, and simmer for 10 minutes (it will not be thoroughly cooked).

In medium bowl, combine water, corn, bell pepper, pimientos, cheese, and 1½ cups of cooked rice. Pour remaining rice into a 9 x 13-inch non-stick, or glass, baking dish and set aside.

Flatten chicken breasts with mallet or back of a wooden spoon. Spread ¼ of rice and corn mixture on each breast, leaving a ¼-inch border on all sides. Roll up each breast beginning with the short side; secure with a toothpick. Sprinkle with pepper to taste.

Place chicken breasts seam side down in the baking dish on top of rice.

Cover and bake for 30 minutes; uncover and continue to bake for an additional 15-20 minutes or until brown.

Remove toothpicks from chicken and cut each roll into 1-inch slices. Serve on top of rice.

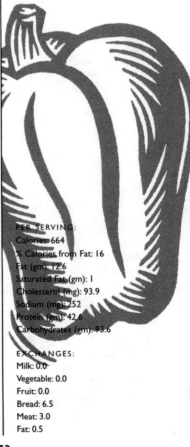

PREPARATION TIME:
20 minutes
COOKING TIME:
45 – 50 minutes
SERVINGS: **4**

PER SERVING:
Calories: 664
% Calories from Fat: 16
Fat (gm): 12.6
Saturated Fat (gm): 1
Cholesterol (mg): 93.9
Sodium (mg): 252
Protein (gm): 42.6
Carbohydrates (gm): 93.6

EXCHANGES:
Milk: 0.0
Vegetable: 0.0
Fruit: 0.0
Bread: 6.5
Meat: 3.0
Fat: 0.5

JAMBALAYA

This Louisiana favorite can't get much easier to prepare while retaining all that Cajun flavor.

PREPARATION TIME:
20 minutes
COOKING TIME:
1 1/2 hours
SERVINGS: **8 – 10**

Vegetable cooking spray
2 cups white rice, uncooked
2 14-ounce packages smoked turkey sausage
1 16-ounce package mushrooms, rinsed and halved
2 large green bell peppers, seeded and coarsely chopped
1 large onion, coarsely chopped
3 celery stalks, coarsely chopped
1 10-ounce package frozen okra
1 4-ounce jar diced pimientos, undrained
2 14$\frac{1}{2}$-ounce cans diced tomatoes, undrained
$\frac{1}{2}$ teaspoon salt
$\frac{1}{2}$ teaspoon cayenne pepper
$\frac{1}{2}$ cup water
1 teaspoon paprika

Preheat oven to 325 degrees.

Coat a 2–2$\frac{1}{2}$-quart casserole with cooking spray. Evenly spread uncooked rice in bottom of dish.

Slice turkey sausage into $\frac{1}{2}$-inch pieces and place in large bowl; add mushrooms, bell peppers, onion, celery, okra, pimientos, tomatoes, salt, and cayenne pepper. Mix well.

Distribute mixture over rice. Pour water over all ingredients in dish and sprinkle with paprika.

Cover tightly and bake for 1$\frac{1}{2}$ hours.

PER SERVING:
Calories: 385
% Calories from Fat: 19
Fat (gm): 8.1
Saturated Fat (gm): 2.1
Cholesterol (mg): 62.9
Sodium (mg): 1160
Protein (gm): 24.3
Carbohydrates (gm): 54.6

EXCHANGES:
Milk: 0.0
Vegetable: 2.0
Fruit: 0.0
Bread: 3.0
Meat: 2.0
Fat: 0.0

WILD RICE CASSEROLE

Although this recipe is meatless, it is hearty and full of flavor. This dish should be accompanied with a salad when serving more than 4 people to make a more complete meal.

PREPARATION TIME:

10 – 15 minutes

COOKING TIME:

55 – 60 minutes

SERVINGS: *4 – 6*

  3 celery stalks, finely chopped
  1 large onion, finely chopped
  1 16-ounce package mushrooms, rinsed and coarsely chopped
  1 15-ounce can tomatoes, crushed and drained
  1 8-ounce can tomato sauce
  1 teaspoon dill seeds
  ½ teaspoon ground thyme
  3 tablespoons soy sauce
  1 egg, beaten
  2 cups (8-ounce package) shredded reduced-fat Cheddar cheese, divided
  1½ cups brown wild rice, uncooked
  1 15½-ounce can dark red kidney beans, well drained

Preheat oven to 350 degrees.

In a large bowl, combine celery, onion, mushrooms, tomatoes, tomato sauce, dill, thyme, soy sauce, egg, and half of the cheese. Mix well.

Stir in the uncooked rice and beans.

Place mixture in a lightly greased round, or oval, casserole (2–2½-quart). Cover and bake for 55 minutes. Uncover and sprinkle with remaining cheese; bake for 5 minutes or until cheese is melted. Serve at once.

PER SERVING:
Calories: 598
% Calories from Fat: 19
Fat (gm): 12.7
Saturated Fat (gm): 5
Cholesterol (mg): 83.6
Sodium (mg): 2473
Protein (gm): 30.3
Carbohydrates (gm): 93.5

EXCHANGES:
Milk: 0.0
Vegetable: 3.0
Fruit: 0.0
Bread: 5.0
Meat: 2.0
Fat: 1.0

MUSHROOM PIE

The combination of portobello and button mushrooms gives this casserole a slightly rich flavor with a hearty texture. To save time, use frozen puff pastry sheets from the freezer section at the grocer (there are two sheets in a box). Don't be intimidated, puff pastry sheets are easy to work with. You can use a pre-formed crust, but I find the type of crust that is unfolded and formed into a baking dish has a much better flavor.

PREPARATION TIME:
20 minutes
COOKING TIME:
45 minutes
SERVINGS: **6**

PIE CRUST

- 2 frozen puff pastry sheets, thawed for 20 minutes at room temperature
- 1 whole egg, lightly beaten, divided

FILLING

- 2 cups brown rice, cooked according to package directions
- 1 16-ounce package mushrooms, halved
- 1 8-ounce package portobello mushrooms, cut into 1-inch pieces
- 1 small white onion, finely chopped
- 1 teaspoon minced garlic
- $\frac{1}{2}$ teaspoon dried dill weed
- 1 tablespoon margarine
- 2 tablespoons flour
- 1 cup low-sodium, fat-free beef broth
- $\frac{1}{2}$ cup dry red wine

Preheat oven to 400 degrees.

PIE CRUST: Unfold one pastry sheet, smooth out with wet fingertips, roll out, and mold to fit bottom of 2-quart oval, or 13 x 9-inch, casserole. Cut three 2-inch slits in bottom of crust to let out steam; otherwise crust will be soggy. Brush with beaten egg. Bake for 15 minutes or until browned. Remove from oven and set aside. Crust will be puffed, but it will deflate a little as it cools. Reduce oven to 350 degrees.

FILLING: In a medium bowl, combine rice, button and portobello mushrooms, onion, garlic, and dill. Set aside.

In a medium saucepan over medium heat, melt the margarine and reduce heat. Add flour, stirring continuously until blended; this smooth mixture is called a roux. Slowly add broth, continually stirring. Increase heat slightly and stir until sauce starts to thicken; add wine while continuing to stir.

Mix sauce with mushrooms and onion. Pour into crust.

Unfold other pastry sheet, smooth out with wet fingertips, and place over filled casserole. Tuck excess pastry inside dish; do not mold around top. With a sharp knife, cut three 2-inch slits into each hemisphere of crust to let steam escape. Brush with beaten egg.

Bake, uncovered, for 30 minutes. Increase oven temperature to 400 degrees and continue to bake for an additional 10 minutes or until crust is golden brown. Let casserole rest for 5 minutes before serving.

PER SERVING:
Calories: 395
% Calories from Fat: 23
Fat (gm): 10.1
Saturated Fat (gm): 1.8
Cholesterol (mg): 35.5
Sodium (mg): 100
Protein (gm): 11.1
Carbohydrates (gm): 62.3

EXCHANGES:
Milk: 0.0
Vegetable: 3.0
Fruit: 0.0
Bread: 3.0
Meat: 0.0
Fat: 2.0

SPICY CHICKEN AND SPANISH RICE

You'll get a taste of the Southwest from this casserole.

2 cups minute, *or* boil-in-bag, rice, uncooked
4 boneless, skinless chicken breast halves, cut into 2-inch pieces
1 14½-ounce can diced tomatoes, undrained
1 8-ounce can tomato sauce
1 10-ounce package frozen corn, thawed and drained
3 tablespoons diced pimientos
1 4-ounce can diced green chilies, drained
¼ teaspoon chili powder
¼ teaspoon ground cumin
⅛ teaspoon cayenne pepper

Preheat oven to 350 degrees.

In a 2½-quart casserole, evenly spread uncooked rice.

Place chicken pieces on top of rice.

In a medium bowl, combine tomatoes, tomato sauce, corn, pimientos, chilies, and spices. Pour mixture over chicken and rice. Stir together.

Cover and bake for 1 hour.

PREPARATION TIME:
20 minutes
COOKING TIME:
1 hour
SERVINGS: **4**

PER SERVING:
Calories: 428
% Calories from Fat: 8
Fat (gm): 3.8
Saturated Fat (gm): 1
Cholesterol (mg): 73
Sodium (mg): 691
Protein (gm): 34.4
Carbohydrates (gm): 64.8

EXCHANGES:
Milk: 0.0
Vegetable: 1.0
Fruit: 0.0
Bread: 3.5
Meat: 3.0
Fat: 0.0

DIJON CHICKEN AU GRATIN

By using pre-packaged individual chicken breast halves, the servings will always come out properly proportioned. These boneless, skinless breasts come in quantities of 9 to 12 in a package, found in the meat section, and are very convenient.

PREPARATION TIME:

15 minutes

COOKING TIME:

45 minutes

SERVINGS: *6*

- 2 cups minute, *or* boil-in-bag, rice (removed from bag), uncooked
- 6 boneless, skinless chicken breast halves
- 1 medium zucchini, cut into $1/4$-inch slices
- 1 large red bell pepper, cut into $1/4$-inch slices
- $1/2$ cup Dijon mustard
- $1/2$ cup white wine
- $1/4$ cup water
- 1 cup unseasoned breadcrumbs
- $1/2$ cup grated Parmesan cheese
- 2 tablespoons dried tarragon

Preheat oven to 350 degrees.

Evenly spread uncooked rice in a 9 x 13-inch non-stick or lightly greased (coat with vegetable cooking spray) glass baking dish. Place chicken breasts on top of rice.

Place zucchini and bell pepper on top of chicken and rice.

In a small bowl, combine Dijon mustard, white wine, and water. Stir until blended and pour over vegetables, chicken, and rice.

Combine breadcrumbs, Parmesan, and tarragon in a small bowl and thoroughly mix together. Sprinkle evenly over entire dish.

Cover and bake for 20 minutes; uncover and bake an additional 25 minutes.

PER SERVING:
Calories: 424
% Calories from Fat: 18
Fat (gm): 8.2
Saturated Fat (gm): 2.9
Cholesterol (mg): 79.6
Sodium (mg): 646
Protein (gm): 37.3
Carbohydrates (gm): 45.5

EXCHANGES:
Milk: 0.0
Vegetable: 0.0
Fruit: 0.0
Bread: 3.0
Meat: 3.0
Fat: 0.0

POLENTA AND CURRIED VEGETABLES

Another time-saver is prepared polenta. Combine that with a medley of frozen vegetables, add some spices and you have a great-tasting meatless meal in minutes.

PREPARATION TIME:
10 minutes
COOKING TIME:
25 minutes
SERVINGS: 4

1	16-ounce package polenta, cut into $1/2$-inch slices
1	16-ounce package frozen mixed vegetables, any variety
1	small onion, finely chopped
2	tablespoons curry powder
$1/2$	teaspoon black pepper, freshly ground, if possible
1	$14^1/_2$-ounce can diced tomatoes, drained

Preheat oven to 350 degrees.

Arrange polenta slices in a 10 x 10-inch baking dish.

In a medium bowl, combine mixed vegetables, onion, curry powder, and black pepper.

Spread vegetable mixture over polenta. Distribute diced tomatoes over vegetable mixture.

Cover and bake for 25 minutes.

PER SERVING:
Calories: 222
% Calories from Fat: 12
Fat (gm): 3.2
Saturated Fat (gm): 0.8
Cholesterol (mg): 2.3
Sodium (mg): 460
Protein (gm): 8.4
Carbohydrates (gm): 43.6

EXCHANGES:
Milk: 0.0
Vegetable: 0.0
Fruit: 0.0
Bread: 3.0
Meat: 0.0
Fat: 0.5

POLLO MOLE (CHICKEN WITH BROWN SAUCE)

*Mole sauce has a distinctive taste unlike most tomato-based sauces tradi-
tionally used in Mexican dishes. I use mole sauce from a can—it is a huge
time-saver over attempting to make it from scratch and still tastes great. This
casserole can be prepared ahead of time and stored in the refrigerator until
ready to bake. If you don't want to pre-bake the onion and peppers, eliminate the oil and increase cooking time by 5 minutes.*

1 large yellow onion, cut into strips

1 large green bell pepper, seeded and cut into strips

1 large red bell pepper, seeded and cut into strips

1 tablespoon light vegetable oil

2 cups long-grain wild rice, cooked *al dente*

1 10-ounce package frozen corn, thawed and drained

1 15-ounce can pinto beans, drained

1 14½-ounce can diced tomatoes, drained

6 boneless, skinless chicken breast halves

1 15-ounce can mole sauce (usually found in ethnic aisle)

1 cup (4-ounce package) shredded reduced-fat Cheddar cheese

Preheat oven to 425 degrees.

Arrange onion and peppers on foil; brush with oil. Place in oven for 10 minutes or
until sizzling. Remove from oven and reduce heat to 350 degrees.

In a 13 x 9-inch glass baking dish, place rice, corn, beans, and tomatoes; mix together.
Place the chicken over rice mixture and arrange the onion and peppers over chicken.
Pour mole sauce evenly over the top.

Cover and bake for 45 minutes; uncover, sprinkle cheese over dish, and continue to
bake for 10 minutes.

PREPARATION TIME:

20 minutes

COOKING TIME:

55 minutes

SERVINGS: **6**

PER SERVING:
Calories: 604
% Calories from Fat: 19
Fat (gm): 12.8
Saturated Fat (gm): 3.2
Cholesterol (mg): 83.1
Sodium (mg): 865
Protein (gm): 47.1
Carbohydrates (gm): 78.8

EXCHANGES:
Milk: 0.0
Vegetable: 2.0
Fruit: 0.0
Bread: 4.0
Meat: 4.0
Fat: 0.5

BEEF AND BROCCOLI TERIYAKI

Meat can be sliced easily after placing it in the freezer for about 20 minutes. For a meatless casserole, substitute tofu for beef. I used a prepared teriyaki mix, to which you simply add water; this reduces sodium by about half.

PREPARATION TIME:
15 minutes

COOKING TIME:
35 minutes

SERVINGS: 4

2 cups minute, *or* boil-in-bag, rice, cooked *al dente*
1 pound beef (sirloin tip, fillet, or round), thinly sliced
1 16-ounce package broccoli, without the stems
1 4-ounce can sliced water chestnuts, with liquid
$\frac{1}{2}$ cup low-sodium teriyaki mix

Preheat oven to 350 degrees.

Evenly spread rice in a 2-quart casserole.

In a large bowl, combine beef, broccoli, water chestnuts, and teriyaki sauce. Pour on top of rice.

Cover and bake for 35 minutes.

PER SERVING:
Calories: 377
% Calories from Fat: 13
Fat (gm): 5.6
Saturated Fat (gm): 2
Cholesterol (mg): 64.9
Sodium (mg): 677
Protein (gm): 29.4
Carbohydrates (gm): 51.5

EXCHANGES:
Milk: 0.0
Vegetable: 2.0
Fruit: 0.0
Bread: 2.0
Meat: 3.0
Fat: 0.0

WILD RICE WITH CHICKEN AND SAUSAGE

Combining chicken and sausage gives this casserole variety and substance, as well as flavor.

$\frac{1}{2}$ pound turkey sausage

1 large yellow onion, minced

3 boneless, skinless chicken breast halves, cut into 1-inch pieces

1 8-ounce package mushrooms, thinly sliced

1 cup light cream

Vegetable cooking spray

2 cups wild rice, cooked *al dente*

$\frac{1}{8}$ teaspoon black pepper, freshly ground, if possible

$\frac{1}{2}$ teaspoon dried ground sage

1 15-ounce can low-sodium, fat-free chicken broth

Preheat oven to 325 degrees.

In a large skillet, break up sausage and brown lightly over medium heat, stirring occasionally. Remove from skillet with a slotted spoon and set on paper towels to absorb excess grease. Drain skillet and saute onion over medium heat until just golden, about 5 minutes.

In a large mixing bowl, combine sausage, onion, chicken, mushrooms, and cream.

Coat a 2-quart casserole with cooking spray. Place rice in casserole and spread meat and mushroom mixture evenly on top.

Sprinkle pepper and sage over the dish and slowly pour in broth.

Bake, uncovered, for 25 minutes. Stir ingredients well and continue to bake for an additional 15 minutes.

PREPARATION TIME:

20 minutes

COOKING TIME:

40 minutes

SERVINGS: **6**

PER SERVING:
Calories: 424
% Calories from Fat: 27
Fat (gm): 12.9
Saturated Fat (gm): 6.1
Cholesterol (mg): 87
Sodium (mg): 392
Protein (gm): 30.8
Carbohydrates (gm): 47.4

EXCHANGES:
Milk: 0.0
Vegetable: 1.0
Fruit: 0.0
Bread: 3.0
Meat: 3.0
Fat: 0.5

BARLEY MUSHROOM BAKE

This meatless casserole is a hearty dish for four or a great side dish for more. Add a salad for a more complete meal.

PREPARATION TIME:
20 minutes

COOKING TIME:
50 minutes

SERVINGS: 4 – 6

1½ cups medium pearl barley
2 tablespoons margarine, divided
1 large yellow onion, minced
1 8-ounce package mushrooms, coarsely chopped
2 13¾-ounce cans low-sodium, fat-free chicken, *or* beef, broth
¼ teaspoon black pepper, freshly ground, if possible

Preheat oven to 350 degrees.

In a medium skillet, stir-fry barley in 1 tablespoon margarine, over medium heat, for about 3 minutes or until lightly browned. Remove from skillet with a slotted spoon and place in a 2-quart casserole.

Using the same skillet, over medium heat saute the onion in remaining margarine until just golden, about 5 minutes. Add mushrooms and continue to saute for an additional 4 minutes.

Spread evenly over barley in casserole. Pour broth over mushrooms and add pepper; mix all ingredients together.

Cover and bake for 50 minutes, stirring midway through, or until barley is tender. Fluff with a fork before serving.

PER SERVING:
Calories: 366
% Calories from Fat: 18
Fat (gm): 7.5
Saturated Fat (gm): 1.3
Cholesterol (mg): 0
Sodium (mg): 137
Protein (gm): 11.3
Carbohydrates (gm): 65.8

EXCHANGES:
Milk: 0.0
Vegetable: 1.0
Fruit: 0.0
Bread: 4.0
Meat: 0.0
Fat: 1.0

SUN-DRIED TOMATO COUSCOUS WITH CHICKEN AND MUSHROOMS

Couscous is the national dish of Morocco. Adding chicken breasts and mushrooms makes this a light and delicious meal.

1 6-ounce package sun-dried tomato couscous (comes in a box with 2 packets)
4 boneless, skinless chicken breast halves
1 16-ounce package mushrooms, cut in halves
1 tablespoon olive oil
1 ½ cups water

Preheat oven to 350 degrees.

Spread couscous and sun-dried tomatoes in a 10 x 10-inch baking dish.

Arrange chicken on top, spread mushrooms over, and drizzle olive oil and water over all.

Cover and bake for 35 minutes.

PREPARATION TIME:
15 minutes
COOKING TIME:
35 minutes
SERVINGS: **4**

PER SERVING:
Calories: 273
% Calories from Fat: 25
Fat (gm): 7.6
Saturated Fat (gm): 1.4
Cholesterol (mg): 73
Sodium (mg): 279
Protein (gm): 32.1
Carbohydrates (gm): 19.9

EXCHANGES:
Milk: 0.0
Vegetable: 1.0
Fruit: 0.0
Bread: 1.0
Meat: 3.0
Fat: 0.0

fast fixes

Spaghetti Bake

The Thing

Tuna Casserole

Pan Pizza Casserole

Quick Chicken and Stuffing

Italian Roll-Ups

Fast Ham and Corn Casserole

Layered Tex-Mex Tortillas

Baked Spinach Mostaccioli

One-Dish Chicken and Rice

Scalloped Ham and Potatoes

Chicken Parmesan

f a s t   f i x e s

SPAGHETTI BAKE

My grandmother made this casserole for me and my sisters when we were kids. Now I make it for my family with a few modifications to reduce calories and fat, plus save time. Try elbow macaroni when making this dish for younger children, as it is easier for them to eat. Make this casserole ahead of time and refrigerate or freeze; then cook for 5 additional minutes (if frozen, thaw in refrigerator before cooking).

PREPARATION TIME:
15 minutes

COOKING TIME:
30 minutes

SERVINGS: *6*

1 pound lean ground beef, cooked and drained
1 16-ounce package spaghetti noodles, cooked *al dente*
2 28-ounce jars spaghetti sauce, any flavor
2 cups (8-ounce package) shredded reduced-fat Cheddar cheese

Preheat oven to 350 degrees.

In a large bowl, combine beef, noodles, and sauce.

Pour spaghetti mixture into a 13 x 9-inch baking dish. Sprinkle cheese over spaghetti, covering evenly.

Bake, uncovered, for 30 minutes.

PER SERVING:
Calories: 854
% Calories from Fat: 29
Fat (gm): 27.7
Saturated Fat (gm): 10.2
Cholesterol (mg): 112
Sodium (mg): 1922
Protein (gm): 36.9
Carbohydrates (gm): 112.7

EXCHANGES:
Milk: 0.0
Vegetable: 0.0
Fruit: 0.0
Bread: 7.0
Meat: 4.0
Fat: 3.0

THE THING

PREPARATION TIME:

15 minutes

COOKING TIME:

20 minutes

SERVINGS: **6**

This casserole has been my favorite "comfort" food since I was 3 years old—and still is. My mom knew it would always "turn my frown upside down." I have modified this quick dish by using reduced-fat cream of mushroom soup. It doesn't get much easier than this! Make this casserole ahead of time and refrigerate or freeze; then cook for 5 additional minutes (if frozen, thaw in refrigerator before cooking).

1	pound lean ground beef, cooked and drained
2	10½-ounce cans reduced-fat cream of mushroom soup
1	16-ounce package elbow macaroni, cooked
1	15-ounce can early peas, drained

Preheat oven to 350 degrees.

In a 2-quart casserole, combine all ingredients and bake for 20 minutes.

PER SERVING:
Calories: 512
% Calories from Fat: 22
Fat (gm): 12.4
Saturated Fat (gm): 4.4
Cholesterol (mg): 48.9
Sodium (mg): 404
Protein (gm): 26.7
Carbohydrates (gm): 71.4

EXCHANGES:
Milk: 0.0
Vegetable: 0.0
Fruit: 0.0
Bread: 5.0
Meat: 2.0
Fat: 1.0

TUNA CASSEROLE

Just like Mom used to make, but with fewer calories and less fat. No-yolk noodles can always be substituted for regular egg noodles to reduce cholesterol.

1   12-ounce package thin egg noodles, uncooked
2   12-ounce cans water-packed white tuna, drained
1   2½-ounce jar diced pimientos
1   8-ounce package mushrooms, rinsed and sliced
1   10½-ounce can reduced-fat cream of mushroom soup
1   10½-ounce can reduced-fat cream of celery soup
½   cup water
½   cup breadcrumbs, seasoned or unseasoned

Preheat oven to 375 degrees.

In a 2–2½-quart casserole, place half of uncooked noodles.

Flake tuna with a fork; do not chop. Layer half each of tuna, pimientos, and mushrooms on top of noodles. Add a layer of remaining noodles and repeat with layer of remaining tuna, pimientos, and mushrooms.

In a small bowl, combine the two cream soups and water. Pour evenly over layered ingredients. Top with breadcrumbs.

Cover and bake for 25 minutes; uncover and bake for an additional 15-20 minutes or until top is brown and bubbling.

PREPARATION TIME:
10 minutes
COOKING TIME
40 – 45 minutes
SERVINGS: **6 – 8**

PER SERVING:
Calories: 447
% Calories from Fat: 13
Fat (gm): 6.5
Saturated Fat (gm): 1.6
Cholesterol (mg): 102.7
Sodium (mg): 927
Protein (gm): 41
Carbohydrates (gm): 53.7

EXCHANGES:
Milk: 0.0
Vegetable: 0.0
Fruit: 0.0
Bread: 3.0
Meat: 4.0
Fat: 0.0

PAN PIZZA CASSEROLE

A fun project for the whole family or a gathering of friends. Use any combination of ingredients—from standards like cheese and sausage to pepperoni, mushrooms, and vegetables.

PREPARATION TIME:

20 minutes

COOKING TIME:

20 minutes

SERVINGS: **6**

1 11-ounce package French bread loaf dough (found in dairy section)
1 8-ounce jar pizza sauce
1 8-ounce package pepperoni slices
1 small green bell pepper, seeded and coarsely chopped
1 small onion, coarsely chopped
2 cups (8-ounce package) shredded reduced-fat mozzarella cheese

Preheat oven to 400 degrees.

Unroll dough into a 13 x 9-inch baking dish; spread dough to cover bottom of dish.

Spoon pizza sauce over dough to thoroughly cover (use more or less depending on taste—there may be sauce left over). Arrange pepperoni on top of sauce. Scatter pepper and onion over pepperoni. Cover with cheese.

Bake, uncovered, for 20 minutes or until cheese is melted and lightly browned.

PER SERVING:
Calories: 498
% Calories from Fat: 45
Fat (gm): 25.4
Saturated Fat (gm): 7
Cholesterol (mg): 17.1
Sodium (mg): 1552
Protein (gm): 25.1
Carbohydrates (gm): 43.8

EXCHANGES:
Milk: 0.0
Vegetable: 0.0
Fruit: 0.0
Bread: 3.0
Meat: 3.0
Fat: 2.5

QUICK CHICKEN AND STUFFING

If time does not permit, substitute half of a 10-ounce package of frozen mixed vegetables for carrots, celery, and onions. Thaw and drain the frozen veggies.

PREPARATION TIME:

15 minutes

COOKING TIME:

30 minutes

SERVINGS: *6*

1 6-ounce package instant chicken-flavored stuffing mix
2 large carrots, coarsely chopped
1 stalk celery, coarsely chopped
1 small onion, finely chopped
1 10½-ounce can reduced-fat cream of mushroom soup
½ cup skim milk
1 teaspoon dried parsley
⅛ teaspoon black pepper, freshly ground, if possible
6 boneless, skinless chicken breast halves
 Paprika, as garnish

Preheat oven to 400 degrees.

In a medium saucepan, prepare stuffing mix according to package directions, but add carrots, celery, and onion (or frozen vegetables) with seasoning packet.

In a small bowl, combine soup, milk, parsley, and black pepper. Set aside.

Place stuffing down center of a 13 x 9-inch baking dish.

Spoon half of soup mixture into baking dish on each side of stuffing. Place chicken breasts over soup, overlapping if necessary. Sprinkle with paprika.

Pour remaining soup mixture over chicken.

Cover and bake 20 minutes; uncover and continue to bake for an additional 10 minutes.

PER SERVING:
Calories: 284
% Calories from Fat: 15
Fat (gm): 4.6
Saturated Fat (gm): 1.3
Cholesterol (mg): 74.4
Sodium (mg): 635
Protein (gm): 31.1
Carbohydrates (gm): 27.2

EXCHANGES:
Milk: 0.0
Vegetable: 1.0
Fruit: 0.0
Bread: 1.5
Meat: 3.0
Fat: 0.0

ITALIAN ROLL-UPS

This is a fun, fast, and easy dish using many ready-made ingredients.

PREPARATION TIME:

15 minutes

COOKING TIME:

30 minutes

SERVINGS: *6 – 8*

1 10-ounce package frozen chopped spinach, thawed and well drained
1 10-ounce package frozen corn, thawed and well drained
1 15-ounce container fat-free ricotta cheese
1 egg
2 cups (8-ounce package) shredded reduced-fat mozzarella cheese, divided
8 flour tortillas
1 14½-ounce can Italian-style diced tomatoes, undrained
1 8-ounce can tomato sauce
1 teaspoon dried basil leaves
¼ cup shredded Parmesan cheese, *or* 2 tablespoons grated Parmesan

Preheat oven to 375 degrees.

In a medium bowl, mix spinach, corn, ricotta, egg, and half of mozzarella until well blended.

Place a heaping one-quarter cup of mixture down center of each tortilla. Roll tightly and arrange seam side down in a 13 x 9-inch baking dish.

In a medium bowl, mix tomatoes, tomato sauce, and basil; spoon over tortillas. Sprinkle with remaining mozzarella and Parmesan cheeses.

Bake, uncovered, 30 minutes.

PER SERVING:
Calories: 390
% Calories from Fat: 21
Fat (gm): 9.6
Saturated Fat (gm): 1.6
Cholesterol (mg): 52.1
Sodium (mg): 953
Protein (gm): 31.2
Carbohydrates (gm): 49.5

EXCHANGES:
Milk: 0.0
Vegetable: 0.0
Fruit: 0.0
Bread: 3.0
Meat: 3.0
Fat: 0.0

FAST HAM AND CORN CASSEROLE

This casserole can be prepared ahead of time and put in the refrigerator or freezer. Cook refrigerated casserole for 5 additional minutes (if frozen, thaw in refrigerator before cooking).

Vegetable cooking spray
3/4 pound cooked lean ham, cut into 1-inch cubes
1 small yellow onion, finely chopped
1 small red bell pepper, seeded and finely chopped
1 15-ounce can cream-style corn
1 10-ounce package frozen corn, thawed and drained
1/2 cup skim milk
1 8-ounce package seasoned bread cubes
3 tablespoons margarine, melted
1 tablespoon Worcestershire sauce

Preheat oven to 350 degrees.

Coat a 2-quart casserole with cooking spray. In casserole, mix ham, onion, bell pepper, cream-style corn, frozen corn, and milk.

Spread bread cubes over top. Add Worcestershire sauce to the melted margarine and drizzle over bread cubes.

Bake, uncovered, 35 minutes or until brown and bubbly.

PREPARATION TIME:
10 minutes
COOKING TIME:
35 minutes
SERVINGS: *4*

PER SERVING:
Calories: 565
% Calories from Fat: 23
Fat (gm): 14.8
Saturated Fat (gm): 3.5
Cholesterol (mg): 26
Sodium (mg): 2926
Protein (gm): 31.9
Carbohydrates (gm): 80.3

EXCHANGES:
Milk: 0.0
Vegetable: 0.0
Fruit: 0.0
Bread: 5.0
Meat: 3.0
Fat: 1.0

LAYERED TEX-MEX TORTILLAS

This casserole has kick! You can control the "temp" by choosing the "degree" of the salsa or by adding sliced jalapeños to the black olives. Olé!

PREPARATION TIME:
20 minutes
COOKING TIME:
35 minutes
SERVINGS: **6 – 8**

1 cup (4-ounce package) shredded fat-free Cheddar cheese
1 cup (4-ounce package) shredded reduced-fat Monterey Jack cheese
1 medium onion, finely chopped
1 medium green bell pepper, seeded, finely chopped
1 garlic clove, minced
3 tablespoons water
1 teaspoon ground cumin
1 teaspoon chili powder
$\frac{3}{4}$ cup mild, medium, *or* hot salsa
1 15-ounce can tomato sauce
1 15-ounce can black beans, drained
1 15-ounce can fat-free pinto beans
12 small (6-inch) corn tortillas
$\frac{3}{4}$ cup fat-free ricotta cheese
1 $2\frac{1}{2}$-ounce can sliced black olives
1 medium tomato, diced
$\frac{1}{2}$ cup fat-free sour cream

Preheat oven to 350 degrees.

Mix the cheeses together in a small bowl and set aside.

In a large mixing bowl, combine onion, bell pepper, garlic, water, ground cumin, chili powder, salsa, and tomato sauce. Mix well. Stir in black beans, then pinto beans, stirring until well blended.

Pour $\frac{1}{3}$ of bean mixture into a $9\frac{1}{2}$ x 13-inch non-stick baking pan, spreading evenly. Place 6 tortillas over mixture, overlapping the edges. Spread ricotta cheese evenly over tortillas. Pour another $\frac{1}{3}$ of bean mixture over ricotta. Top with $\frac{1}{2}$ of the combined cheeses and cover with sliced olives. Place remaining tortillas over olives, and then add the remaining bean mixture.

Cover and bake for 30 minutes or until thoroughly heated. Uncover, sprinkle on the remaining cheese, and bake until melted, 5 or 6 minutes.

Cut into rectangular pieces and garnish with diced tomatoes and sour cream.

PER SERVING:
Calories: 442
% Calories from Fat: 19
Fat (gm): 10.4
Saturated Fat (gm): 2.7
Cholesterol (mg): 13.5
Sodium (mg): 1919
Protein (gm): 33.2
Carbohydrates (gm): 65.5

EXCHANGES:
Milk: 0.0
Vegetable: 0.0
Fruit: 0.0
Bread: 4.0
Meat: 2.0
Fat: 1.0

BAKED SPINACH MOSTACCIOLI

Great for a block party, picnic, or family gathering, this casserole is quick and easy to make using ingredients that are stock items in most kitchens. This casserole can be prepared ahead of time and put in the refrigerator or freezer. Cook refrigerated casserole for 5 additional minutes (if frozen, thaw in refrigerator before cooking).

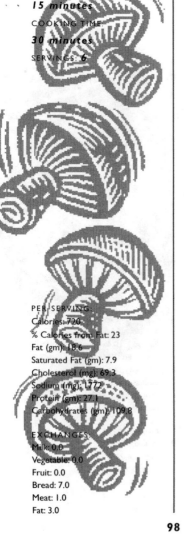

PREPARATION TIME:
15 minutes

COOKING TIME:
30 minutes

SERVINGS: *6*

1 16-ounce package mostaccioli noodles, cooked *al dente*
1 10-ounce package frozen chopped spinach, thawed and drained
1 8-ounce package mushrooms, halved
2 28-ounce jars spaghetti sauce, any flavor
2 cups (8-ounce package) shredded reduced-fat mozzarella cheese

Preheat oven to 350 degrees.

Place half the noodles in a 2½-quart casserole. Spread spinach and mushrooms over noodles and arrange remaining noodles over vegetables.

Pour sauce over all and sprinkle with cheese.

Cover and bake for 30 minutes.

PER SERVING:
Calories: 720
% Calories from Fat: 23
Fat (gm): 18.6
Saturated Fat (gm): 7.9
Cholesterol (mg): 69.3
Sodium (mg): 1772
Protein (gm): 27.1
Carbohydrates (gm): 109.8

EXCHANGES:
Milk: 0.0
Vegetable: 0.0
Fruit: 0.0
Bread: 7.0
Meat: 1.0
Fat: 3.0

ONE-DISH CHICKEN AND RICE

This casserole can be prepared ahead of time and put in the refrigerator or freezer. Cook refrigerated casserole for 5-10 additional minutes to ensure that chicken is cooked properly (if frozen, thaw in refrigerator before cooking).

PREPARATION TIME:

10 minutes

COOKING TIME:

45 minutes

SERVINGS: **4**

1   10½-ounce can reduced-fat cream of mushroom soup
¾   cup skim milk
¾   cup long-grain rice, uncooked
¼   teaspoon paprika, divided
¼   teaspoon white pepper, divided
½   teaspoon dried tarragon
1   10-ounce package frozen cut green beans
4   boneless, skinless chicken breast halves

Preheat oven to 375 degrees.

In a 2-quart shallow baking dish (about 9 inches diameter), mix soup, milk, rice, half of paprika, half of pepper, tarragon, and green beans.

Place chicken over rice mixture; sprinkle with remaining paprika and pepper.

Cover and bake for 45 minutes or until bubbly.

PER SERVING:
Calories: 332
% Calories from Fat: 12
Fat (gm): 4.2
Saturated Fat (gm): 1.2
Cholesterol (mg): 75.4
Sodium (mg): 247
Protein (gm): 32
Carbohydrates (gm): 37.1

EXCHANGES:
Milk: 0.0
Vegetable: 1.0
Fruit: 0.0
Bread: 2.0
Meat: 3.0
Fat: 0.0

SCALLOPED HAM AND POTATOES

This casserole is another childhood favorite. I have modified the recipe to lower calories and fat by using margarine and reduced-fat cheese.

PREPARATION TIME:
15 minutes
COOKING TIME:
30 minutes
SERVINGS: 6

Vegetable cooking spray
4 medium potatoes, peeled and very thinly sliced
1 pound cooked lean ham, cut into 1-inch cubes
1 medium white onion, thinly sliced
2 tablespoons margarine
$1/4$ teaspoon lemon pepper
$1/2$ teaspoon salt
1 10-ounce package frozen cut carrots
1 cup (4-ounce package) shredded reduced-fat Cheddar cheese
1 cup skim milk

Preheat oven to 350 degrees.

Coat a 13 x 9-inch baking dish with cooking spray.

Put potatoes in a large, shallow microwave-safe dish, cover with a wet paper towel, and cook on high for 3 minutes. Stir potatoes and cook for an additional 4 minutes or until potatoes are soft.

Alternately layer potatoes, ham, onions (dot each onion layer with margarine and sprinkle with lemon pepper and salt), carrots, and cheese in baking dish, beginning and ending with potatoes.

Pour in milk when all ingredients are layered.

Cover and bake for 30 minutes.

PER SERVING
Calories: 329
% Calories from Fat: 29
Fat (gm): 10.4
Saturated Fat (gm): 3.4
Cholesterol (mg): 33.5
Sodium (mg): 1392
Protein (gm): 24.5
Carbohydrates (gm): 34.2

EXCHANGES
Milk: 0.0
Vegetable: 0.0
Fruit: 0.0
Bread: 2.0
Meat: 3.0
Fat: 0.5

CHICKEN PARMESAN

This fast-fix casserole, using frozen breaded chicken breast halves, a flavorful jar of mushroom spaghetti sauce, and a few fresh mushrooms, is a real treat that no one will believe wasn't freshly prepared.

1 16-ounce package thin spaghetti noodles, cooked *al dente*
2 9-ounce packages frozen breaded chicken breast halves
8 large mushrooms, thickly sliced
1 28-ounce jar mushroom spaghetti sauce
1 cup (4-ounce package) shredded reduced-fat mozzarella cheese
1/4 cup grated Parmesan cheese

Preheat oven to 350 degrees.

Place noodles in a 2-quart casserole. Then arrange chicken and mushrooms on top of noodles.

Pour sauce evenly over the casserole. Sprinkle mozzarella and Parmesan over sauce.

Cook, uncovered, for 30 minutes or until cheese is bubbly and browned.

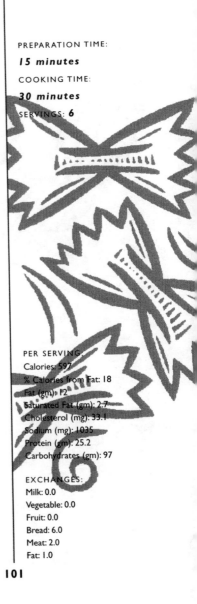

PREPARATION TIME:
15 minutes
COOKING TIME:
30 minutes
SERVINGS: **6**

PER SERVING:
Calories: 597
% Calories from Fat: 18
Fat (gm): 12
Saturated Fat (gm): 2.7
Cholesterol (mg): 33.1
Sodium (mg): 1035
Protein (gm): 25.2
Carbohydrates (gm): 97

EXCHANGES:
Milk: 0.0
Vegetable: 0.0
Fruit: 0.0
Bread: 6.0
Meat: 2.0
Fat: 1.0

simply
side
dishes

Zucchini Casserole

Green Bean Bake

Corn Bread Casserole

Sweet Potato Casserole

Baked Taco Dip

Salmon Salad

Broccoli Casserole

Rice Dressing

Artichokes Parmesan

Garlic-Cheddar Mashed Potato Bake

Baked Spanish Rice with Cheese

Scalloped Potatoes

Asparagus and Cheese Casserole

Vegetables au Gratin

ZUCCHINI CASSEROLE

There's just no way around using a can of cream soup in this recipe—it gives the casserole the right consistency. I have tried other methods, but this one is best for this side dish.

- 4   medium zucchini, cubed
- 2   large carrots, shredded
- 1   cup (8-ounces) fat-free sour cream
- 1 $10\frac{1}{2}$-ounce can reduced-fat cream of chicken soup
- $\frac{1}{4}$ teaspoon black pepper, freshly ground, if possible
- 2   tablespoons diced pimientos
- 1   small onion, finely chopped
- 1   8-ounce package seasoned bread cubes
- 4   tablespoons ($\frac{1}{2}$ stick) margarine, melted
- $\frac{1}{2}$ cup warm water

Preheat oven to 350 degrees.

In a large mixing bowl, combine zucchini, carrots, sour cream, soup, pepper, pimientos, and onion. Set aside.

In a $2-2\frac{1}{2}$-quart casserole, mix bread cubes, margarine, and water. Remove half of the bread cubes mixture and set aside.

Spoon the zucchini mixture over the bread cubes and spread evenly to cover. Place the remaining bread cubes on top to cover zucchini mixture.

Cover and bake 25 minutes; remove cover and continue to bake for an additional 20 minutes or until browned.

PREPARATION TIME:
20 minutes
COOKING TIME:
45 minutes
SERVINGS: *6 – 8*

PER SERVING:
Calories: 291
% Calories from Fat: 30
Fat (gm): 10.4
Saturated Fat (gm): 2.4
Cholesterol (mg): 6.2
Sodium (mg): 1519
Protein (gm): 10.7
Carbohydrates (gm): 40.6

EXCHANGES:
Milk: 0.0
Vegetable: 2.0
Fruit: 0.0
Bread: 2.0
Meat: 0.0
Fat: 2.0

GREEN BEAN BAKE

This classic side dish is a mainstay of every family's holiday menu. There is no getting around the fact that cream of mushroom soup must be used to keep the flavor we all know and maintain the simplicity of this casserole. Recipe can be doubled for larger gatherings (use 2½-quart casserole).

PREPARATION TIME:
10 minutes
COOKING TIME:
30 minutes
SERVINGS: **6**

2 10½-ounce cans reduced-fat cream of mushroom soup
½ cup skim milk
1 teaspoon Worcestershire sauce
⅛ teaspoon black pepper, freshly ground, if possible
1 16-ounce package frozen French-cut green beans, cooked and drained
1 small can (2.8 ounces) French-fried onions, divided

Preheat oven to 350 degrees.

In a 1½-quart casserole, combine soup, milk, Worcestershire, and pepper. Stir in beans and half of the fried onions.

Bake, uncovered, for 20 minutes. Top with remaining fried onions and continue to bake for an additional 10 minutes.

PER SERVING:
Calories: 63
% Calories from Fat: 25
Fat (gm): 1.8
Saturated Fat (gm): 0.5
Cholesterol (mg): 2.5
Sodium (mg): 243
Protein (gm): 2.1
Carbohydrates (gm): 10

EXCHANGES:
Milk: 0.0
Vegetable: 2.0
Fruit: 0.0
Bread: 0.0
Meat: 0.0
Fat: 0.5

CORN BREAD CASSEROLE

This old-fashioned favorite has been updated by adding onion and Cheddar cheese. If you want to add a little zing to this bread, mix a few finely chopped jalapeño peppers in with the onions. It is a great side dish to accompany chili.

PREPARATION TIME:
10 – 15 minutes
COOKING TIME:
35 – 40 minutes
SERVINGS: *6 – 8*

4 tablespoons margarine

2 medium onions, finely chopped

2 large eggs

2 tablespoons skim milk

2 15-ounce cans cream-style corn (low-sodium, if desired)

1 1-pound package cornmeal muffin mix
Vegetable cooking spray

1 8-ounce container reduced-fat, *or* fat-free, sour cream, *or* yogurt
1 cup (4-ounce package) shredded reduced-fat Cheddar cheese
(set aside $\frac{1}{4}$ cup for topping)

Preheat oven to 350 degrees.

In a medium saute pan or skillet, melt margarine and cook onions over medium heat until slightly golden brown; remove from heat. Set aside.

In a large mixing bowl, combine eggs and milk, stirring until blended. Add creamed corn and muffin mix, and continue to stir until well blended and creamy (you may have very small lumps).

Coat a 9 x 13-inch oval casserole with cooking spray. Spread layer of batter, then add a layer of each: onions, sour cream or yogurt, and cheese. Continue to layer in the same order until ingredients are gone, about three layers. Top with $\frac{1}{4}$ cup of remaining cheese.

Bake 35-40 minutes or until puffed and golden. Let stand for 10 minutes before cutting. Serve warm or at room temperature.

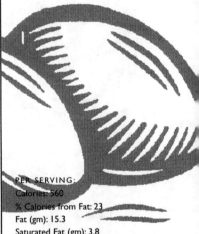

PER SERVING:
Calories: 560
% Calories from Fat: 23
Fat (gm): 15.3
Saturated Fat (gm): 3.8
Cholesterol (mg): 81.2
Sodium (mg): 826
Protein (gm): 18.1
Carbohydrates (gm): 94.1

EXCHANGES:
Milk: 0.0
Vegetable: 0.0
Fruit: 0.0
Bread: 6.0
Meat: 1.0
Fat: 2.0

SWEET POTATO CASSEROLE

A modern version of the old-fashioned side-dish that has all the slow-cooked richness without the fat. This dish allows you a lot of spare time while it bakes in the oven. The casserole can be prepared ahead of time and refrigerated, but add 15 minutes to initial baking time.

PREPARATION TIME:

20 minutes

COOKING TIME:

2 hours

SERVINGS: **6**

Vegetable cooking spray

4 large sweet potatoes, peeled and cut into $\frac{1}{8}$-inch slices

$\frac{1}{4}$ cup low-sodium, fat-free chicken broth

$\frac{1}{4}$ cup honey

2 tablespoons lemon juice

1 tablespoon canola oil, *or other very light oil*

$\frac{1}{2}$ teaspoon salt

$\frac{1}{2}$ teaspoon ground ginger

$\frac{1}{2}$ teaspoon ground nutmeg

$\frac{1}{4}$ teaspoon black pepper, freshly ground, if possible

Preheat oven to 350 degrees.

Heavily coat a 2-quart baking dish with cooking spray.

Layer sweet potato slices in the dish.

In a small bowl, combine all remaining ingredients and mix well. Pour over the sweet potatoes.

Cover tightly and bake for $1\frac{1}{2}$ hours until the sweet potatoes are very tender. Uncover and continue to bake, basting often (every 5-10 minutes), until the liquid has reduced to a syrup consistency and the top is glazed, about 30 minutes.

PER SERVING:
Calories: 145
% Calories from Fat: 15
Fat (gm): 2.5
Saturated Fat (gm): 0.2
Cholesterol (mg): 0
Sodium (mg): 189
Protein (gm): 1.5
Carbohydrates (gm): 30.6

EXCHANGES:
Milk: 0.0
Vegetable: 0.0
Fruit: 0.0
Bread: 2.0
Meat: 0.0
Fat: 0.5

BAKED TACO DIP

This is a hearty dip, using low-fat ingredients, that is great for any occasion. For a meatless version, you can eliminate the beef and add an additional can of refried beans. Serve with tortilla chips.

- 1 pound lean ground beef
- 1 small onion, finely chopped
- 1 16-ounce can fat-free refried beans, divided
- 1 4-ounce can diced green chilies, drained, divided
- 1 8-ounce jar mild, medium, or hot salsa, divided
- 2 cups (8-ounce package) shredded reduced-fat Cheddar cheese, divided
- 1 8-ounce container fat-free sour cream
- $1/3$ cup (about 3 stems) chopped green onions
- 1 $2^1/_2$-ounce can chopped black olives
  Tortilla chips, to taste, for dipping

Preheat oven to 350 degrees.

Using a large skillet, cook beef and onion, stirring occasionally, until browned; drain.

Spoon half of beans into 13 x 9-inch glass baking dish. Top with half each of meat, chilies, salsa, and cheese. Repeat with remaining beans, meat, chilies, salsa, and cheese.

Bake, uncovered, for 30 minutes or until cheese is melted.

Top with sour cream, green onions, and olives. Serve with tortilla chips.

PREPARATION TIME:
15 minutes
COOKING TIME:
30 minutes
SERVINGS: *6 – 8*

PER SERVING:
Calories: 356
% Calories from Fat: 45
Fat (gm): 17.9
Saturated Fat (gm): 6.9
Cholesterol (mg): 66.9
Sodium (mg): 1289
Protein (gm): 28.1
Carbohydrates (gm): 21.7

EXCHANGES:
Milk: 0.0
Vegetable: 0.0
Fruit: 0.0
Bread: 1.5
Meat: 3.0
Fat: 2.0

SALMON SALAD

A light, colorful cold casserole that is an elegant side dish for a luncheon or shower.

PREPARATION TIME:
20 minutes
REFRIGERATION TIME:
I hour
SERVINGS: **6**

1 14¾-ounce can boneless, skinless salmon, drained
1 8-ounce package small shell macaroni, cooked
1 large carrot, thinly sliced
1 celery stalk, thinly sliced
1 tablespoon olive oil
½ cup fat-free mayonnaise, *or* salad dressing
½ cup fat-free ranch dressing
2 green onion stalks, cut into 1-inch pieces
1 small green bell pepper, thinly sliced
1 medium tomato, seeded and chopped
1 4-ounce can sliced black olives
⅛ teaspoon black pepper, freshly ground, if possible

In a 2½-quart casserole, combine salmon, macaroni, carrots, celery, and olive oil; mix well.

In a small bowl, mix salad dressing and ranch dressing. Stir into salmon mixture.

Arrange green onion, green pepper, tomato, and olives on top of salad. Sprinkle with black pepper.

Refrigerate for 1 hour.

PER SERVING:
Calories: 397
% Calories from Fat: 35
Fat (gm): 15.4
Saturated Fat (gm): 2.4
Cholesterol (mg): 33
Sodium (mg): 1494
Protein (gm): 21.3
Carbohydrates (gm): 42.2

EXCHANGES:
Milk: 0.0
Vegetable: 0.0
Fruit: 0.0
Bread: 3.0
Meat: 2.0
Fat: 2.0

BROCCOLI CASSEROLE

There is no better combination than broccoli and cheese. Add chicken breasts to this dish and you have a complete meal.

- 1   16-ounce package frozen broccoli cuts, thawed and drained
- 2   stalks celery, coarsely chopped
- 1   small onion, coarsely chopped
- 1   8-ounce package mushrooms, coarsely chopped
- 2   cups minute, *or* boil-in-bag, rice, cooked according to package directions
- 1   cup (4-ounce package) shredded reduced-fat Cheddar cheese
- 1   cup (4-ounce package) shredded reduced-fat mozzarella cheese
- 1   13¾-ounce can low-sodium, fat-free vegetable broth
- 1½ cups unseasoned breadcrumbs

Preheat oven to 375 degrees.

In a 2½-quart casserole, combine broccoli, celery, onion, mushrooms, rice, and cheeses. Mix together well.

Pour broth over entire mixture. Sprinkle breadcrumbs evenly over top.

Bake, uncovered, for 50 minutes or until bubbly and browned.

PREPARATION TIME:
15 minutes
COOKING TIME:
50 minutes
SERVINGS: 6

PER SERVING:
Calories: 362
% Calories from Fat: 16
Fat (gm): 6.5
Saturated Fat (gm): 1.8
Cholesterol (mg): 16.8
Sodium (mg): 648
Protein (gm): 18.8
Carbohydrates (gm): 57.9

EXCHANGES:
Milk: 0.0
Vegetable: 2.0
Fruit: 0.0
Bread: 3.0
Meat: 1.0
Fat: 0.0

RICE DRESSING

*With turkey, pork, or beef, this dish can be the perfect accompaniment.
Or, serve as a light alternative main dish with a salad or other side dish.
Use boil-in-bag rice to save time, but be sure not to overcook.*

PREPARATION TIME:
15 minutes
COOKING TIME:
40 minutes
SERVINGS: 6 – 8

1 pound ground pork, beef, *or* turkey
1 tablespoon minced garlic
1 small onion, finely chopped
2 celery stalks, finely chopped
1 8-ounce package mushrooms, rinsed and coarsely chopped
2 tablespoons Worcestershire sauce
6 cups instant rice, cooked according to package directions
1 teaspoon black pepper, freshly ground, if possible
1 teaspoon salt
1 1/2 teaspoons cayenne pepper
1/2 cup fresh parsley, chopped (1/4 cup dried parsley can be substituted)

Preheat oven to 350 degrees.

In a large saute pan or skillet, brown ground meat with the garlic over medium heat.
Drain excess liquid.

Place the onion, celery, mushrooms, and Worcestershire sauce in a 2–2 1/2-quart
casserole; stir in cooked rice and meat. Sprinkle salt, pepper, cayenne pepper, and
parsley over mixture.

Cover and bake for 40 minutes.

PER SERVING:
Calories: 507
% Calories from Fat: 10
Fat (gm): 5.4
Saturated Fat (gm): 1.8
Cholesterol (mg): 42.9
Sodium (mg): 474
Protein (gm): 27.1
Carbohydrates (gm): 84.7

EXCHANGES:
Milk: 0.0
Vegetable: 0.0
Fruit: 0.0
Bread: 5.5
Meat: 2.0
Fat: 0.0

ARTICHOKES PARMESAN

A delicious light-tasting side dish that is great for lunch or dinner.

- 1 16-ounce package frozen artichokes, thawed and drained
- 1 tablespoon lemon juice
- 1 stalk green onion, thinly sliced
- 1 teaspoon minced garlic
- 1 14½-ounce can diced tomatoes, drained
- 2 cups seasoned breadcrumbs
- ¼ cup grated Parmesan cheese
- 2 tablespoons dried parsley

Preheat oven to 350 degrees.

In a 10 x 10-inch baking dish, space artichokes evenly.

In a small bowl, combine lemon juice, green onion, garlic, and tomatoes. Pour over artichokes.

Cover ingredients with breadcrumbs. Sprinkle with Parmesan cheese and parsley.

Cover and bake for 25 minutes; uncover and continue to bake for an additional 10 minutes.

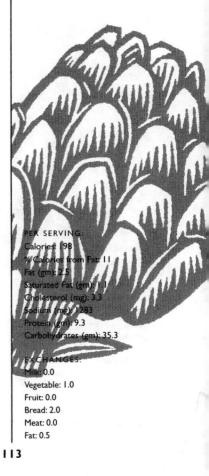

PREPARATION TIME:

15 minutes

COOKING TIME:

35 minutes

SERVINGS: **6**

PER SERVING:
Calories: 198
% Calories from Fat: 11
Fat (gm): 2.5
Saturated Fat (gm): 1.1
Cholesterol (mg): 3.3
Sodium (mg): 1283
Protein (gm): 9.3
Carbohydrates (gm): 35.3

EXCHANGES:
Milk: 0.0
Vegetable: 1.0
Fruit: 0.0
Bread: 2.0
Meat: 0.0
Fat: 0.5

GARLIC-CHEDDAR MASHED POTATO BAKE

A lot of garlic is a must in this hearty side dish.

PREPARATION TIME:
20 minutes
COOKING TIME:
30 minutes
SERVINGS: **8**

2 pounds russet potatoes, peeled, cut into eighths
6 large garlic cloves
$\frac{1}{2}$ teaspoon salt
$\frac{3}{4}$ cup skim milk, heated
2 tablespoons margarine, softened
1 tablespoon chives, coarsely chopped
$\frac{1}{8}$ teaspoon white pepper
2 cups (8-ounce package) shredded reduced-fat Cheddar cheese, divided

Preheat oven to 350 degrees.

Place potatoes in a large saucepan; cover with cold water. Add garlic and salt; cover and bring to a boil. Remove cover and boil 15 minutes or until potatoes are tender. Drain and mash.

Stir in milk, margarine, chives, and pepper.

Gradually add half of cheese, stirring until blended.

Spoon into 2-quart casserole and top with remaining cheese. Cover and bake for 30 minutes.

PER SERVING:
Calories: 217
% Calories from Fat: 29
Fat (gm): 7.1
Saturated Fat (gm): 2.6
Cholesterol (mg): 15.6
Sodium (mg): 569
Protein (gm): 9.4
Carbohydrates (gm): 29.4

EXCHANGES:
Milk: 0.0
Vegetable: 0.0
Fruit: 0.0
Bread: 2.0
Meat: 1.0
Fat: 0.5

BAKED SPANISH RICE WITH CHEESE

A Southwestern-style side dish with just the right spice.

Vegetable cooking spray
1 medium yellow onion, minced
1 small green bell pepper, seeded and minced
1 small red bell pepper, seeded and minced
1/4 teaspoon chili powder
1/8 teaspoon ground cumin
1 cup minute, *or* boil-in-bag, rice, cooked *al dente*
1 14 1/2-ounce can diced tomatoes, undrained
1 bay leaf, crumbled
1/8 teaspoon salt
1/8 teaspoon black pepper, freshly ground, if possible
1 cup (4-ounce package) shredded reduced-fat Cheddar cheese

Preheat oven to 350 degrees.

Coat a medium skillet with cooking spray. Over medium heat, saute onion and green and red peppers for about 4 minutes. Stir in chili powder and cumin.

Place rice in a 2-quart casserole, and spoon in the onion and peppers mixture.

Pour in tomatoes; add the bay leaf, salt, pepper, and cheese. Lightly mix together all ingredients.

Cover and bake for 35 minutes.

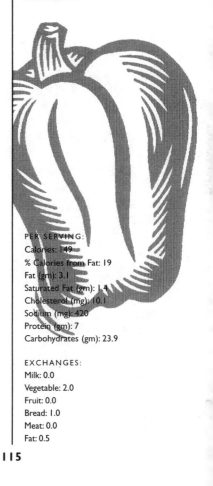

PREPARATION TIME:
15 minutes
COOKING TIME:
35 minutes
SERVINGS: **6**

PER SERVING:
Calories: 149
% Calories from Fat: 19
Fat (gm): 3.1
Saturated Fat (gm): 1.4
Cholesterol (mg): 10.1
Sodium (mg): 420
Protein (gm): 7
Carbohydrates (gm): 23.9

EXCHANGES:
Milk: 0.0
Vegetable: 2.0
Fruit: 0.0
Bread: 1.0
Meat: 0.0
Fat: 0.5

SCALLOPED POTATOES

A classic family favorite made lower in fat by using margarine, skim milk, and reduced-fat cheese. There really is no way to prepare this dish faster yet keep the nostalgic flavor that everyone loves. This dish can be prepared ahead of time and refrigerated before baking. No additional cooking time is then necessary.

PREPARATION TIME:

15 minutes

COOKING TIME:

**1 hour,
15 – 20 minutes**

SERVINGS: **6**

Vegetable cooking spray
6 medium potatoes, peeled and very thinly sliced
2 small white onions, sliced paper thin
2 cups (8-ounce package) shredded reduced-fat Cheddar cheese
4 tablespoons margarine
$\frac{1}{4}$ teaspoon dried dill
$\frac{1}{4}$ teaspoon lemon pepper
$\frac{1}{2}$ teaspoon salt
$1\frac{1}{2}$ cups skim milk

Preheat oven to 325 degrees.

Coat a $2\frac{1}{2}$-quart casserole with cooking spray. Alternately layer potatoes, onions, and cheese, beginning and ending with potatoes.

Dot each onion layer with margarine and sprinkle with dill, lemon pepper, and salt. Pour in milk when all ingredients are layered.

Cover and bake 45 minutes; uncover and bake for an additional 30-35 minutes or until potatoes are tender and almost all liquid is absorbed. If you would like the top very brown, broil for 2-3 minutes before serving.

PER SERVING:
Calories: 339
% Calories from Fat: 35
Fat (gm): 13.3
Saturated Fat (gm): 4.3
Cholesterol (mg): 21.3
Sodium (mg): 819
Protein (gm): 13.7
Carbohydrates (gm): 41.7

EXCHANGES:
Milk: 0.0
Vegetable: 0.0
Fruit: 0.0
Bread: 2.5
Meat: 1.0
Fat: 2.0

ASPARAGUS AND CHEESE CASSEROLE

Fresh asparagus is the best choice for this creamy casserole.

- 5 tablespoons margarine, reserving 1 tablespoon
- 6 tablespoons flour
- 2 cups skim milk
- 1/8 teaspoon salt
- 1/8 teaspoon white pepper
- 2 cups (8-ounce package) shredded reduced-fat Cheddar cheese, divided
- 2 pounds fresh asparagus, steamed, *or* 2 10-ounce packages frozen asparagus, cooked; reserve 1 cup liquid
- 1 cup unseasoned breadcrumbs

Preheat oven to 375 degrees.

In a medium saucepan, melt 4 tablespoons of margarine over medium heat and blend in flour. Add the cup of liquid from the asparagus and milk and heat, stirring constantly, until thickened.

Add salt, pepper, and 1 cup of cheese; over same heat, stir until cheese is melted. Remove from heat.

Arrange asparagus in a shallow 2-quart casserole and top with cheese sauce. Toss remaining cheese with breadcrumbs, sprinkle over sauce, and dot with remaining tablespoon of margarine.

Bake, uncovered, 20 minutes or until bubbly and lightly browned.

PREPARATION TIME:
15 minutes
COOKING TIME:
20 minutes
SERVINGS: **4**

PER SERVING:
Calories: 511
% Calories from Fat: 43
Fat (gm): 24.7
Saturated Fat (gm): 7.5
Cholesterol (mg): 32.4
Sodium (mg): 1320
Protein (gm): 26.5
Carbohydrates (gm): 47.6

EXCHANGES:
Milk: 0.0
Vegetable: 3.0
Fruit: 0.0
Bread: 2.0
Meat: 2.0
Fat: 4.0

VEGETABLES AU GRATIN

Any combination of vegetables will work well in this recipe. Using frozen veggies saves a lot of preparation as well as cooking time without sacrificing flavor.

PREPARATION TIME:

15 minutes

COOKING TIME:

35 minutes

SERVINGS: *8*

Vegetable cooking spray

2 10-ounce packages frozen mixed vegetables, thawed and drained

1 small onion, julienned

2 tablespoons margarine

3 tablespoons flour

2 cups skim milk

$1/8$ teaspoon black pepper, freshly ground, if possible

$1/4$ teaspoon paprika

1 cup (4-ounce package) shredded reduced-fat Cheddar cheese

$1/2$ cup unseasoned breadcrumbs

Preheat oven to 350 degrees.

Lightly coat a 2-quart casserole with cooking spray and spread mixed vegetables in dish. Place julienned onion on top of vegetables.

In a small saucepan over medium heat, melt margarine and blend in flour. Slowly add milk and continue to stir over medium heat until sauce thickens; mix in pepper and paprika. Pour sauce evenly over vegetables.

Sprinkle cheese and breadcrumbs evenly over sauce.

Cover and bake for 25 minutes; uncover and continue to bake for an additional 10 minutes or until top is browned.

PER SERVING:
Calories: 157
% Calories from Fat: 30
Fat (gm): 5.4
Saturated Fat (gm): 1.7
Cholesterol (mg): 8.6
Sodium (mg): 420
Protein (gm): 8.1
Carbohydrates (gm): 19.6

EXCHANGES:
Milk: 0.0
Vegetable: 2.0
Fruit: 0.0
Bread: 0.5
Meat: 1.0
Fat: 0.5

brunch
and light
dishes

Huevos Rancheros

Denver Omelette Casserole

Tomato and Vegetable Quiche

French Toast Casserole

Strawberry-Banana Torte

Easy Cheese Puff

Egg and Broccoli Casserole

HUEVOS RANCHEROS

This Mexican classic is a skillet casserole. It is full of flavor, using prepared salsa, and is a quick and easy brunch dish. Always use fresh eggs, they taste best. A way to tell if eggs are fresh is by placing them in a bowl of cold water. The ones that float are not usable.

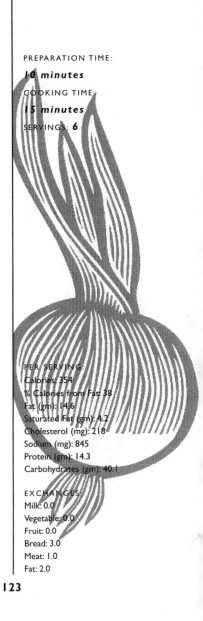

6 large wheat flour tortillas
2 tablespoons margarine
1 small yellow onion, finely chopped
6 eggs, slightly beaten, *or* egg substitute
1 cup prepared salsa, in desired spiciness
¼ teaspoon chili powder
½ cup (2 ounces) shredded reduced-fat Cheddar cheese

Preheat oven to 200 degrees.

Wrap tortillas in foil and place in oven to warm while preparing eggs.

In a large skillet, melt margarine and saute onions over medium heat for 3-4 minutes. Pour in eggs and scramble, stirring continuously until fluffy. Before eggs are entirely done, stir in salsa and chili powder.

Remove tortillas from oven and place on plates. Spoon eggs onto each tortilla and sprinkle with cheese. Serve immediately.

PREPARATION TIME:
10 minutes
COOKING TIME:
15 minutes
SERVINGS: **6**

PER SERVING:
Calories: 354
% Calories from Fat: 38
Fat (gm): 14.6
Saturated Fat (gm): 4.2
Cholesterol (mg): 218
Sodium (mg): 845
Protein (gm): 14.3
Carbohydrates (gm): 40.1

EXCHANGES:
Milk: 0.0
Vegetable: 0.0
Fruit: 0.0
Bread: 3.0
Meat: 1.0
Fat: 2.0

DENVER OMELETTE CASSEROLE

My version of this breakfast classic contains mushrooms and cheese. To lower calories, cholesterol, and fat, use egg substitute equivalent to 4 eggs instead of eggs and egg whites.

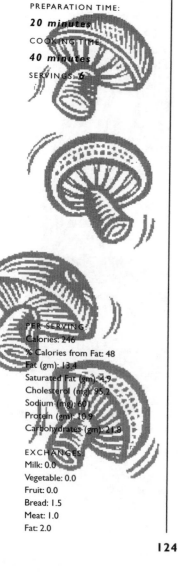

PREPARATION TIME:

20 minutes

COOKING TIME

40 minutes

SERVINGS: 6

- 1 7½-ounce package buttermilk biscuits, uncooked (found in dairy section)
- 2 tablespoons margarine
- 1 medium onion, finely chopped
- ½ large green bell pepper, finely sliced
- ½ large red bell pepper, finely sliced
- 8 medium mushrooms, sliced
- 2 egg whites
- ¼ cup heavy cream
- ¾ cup skim milk
- ½ tablespoon dried parsley
- Salt and pepper to taste
- 2 large whole eggs
- 1 cup (4-ounce package) shredded reduced-fat Cheddar cheese

Preheat oven to 350 degrees.

Separate biscuits and place in ungreased 8- or 9-inch pie pan or quiche dish. Press edges of biscuits together to line the pan.

Melt margarine in a saute pan or skillet, add onion, peppers, and mushrooms, and cook over low heat until vegetables are just softened (about 4 minutes). Spread vegetables over biscuits.

Beat egg whites until frothy, add cream, milk, parsley, salt, pepper, and then whole eggs. Pour over the vegetables and sprinkle cheese on top.

Bake for 40 minutes or until top is golden brown. Test by inserting knife into center; if knife is not coated, omelette should be done.

PER SERVING
Calories: 246
% Calories from Fat: 48
Fat (gm): 13.4
Saturated Fat (gm): 4.9
Cholesterol (mg): 95.2
Sodium (mg): 601
Protein (gm): 10.9
Carbohydrates (gm): 21.8

EXCHANGES:
Milk: 0.0
Vegetable: 0.0
Fruit: 0.0
Bread: 1.5
Meat: 1.0
Fat: 2.0

TOMATO AND VEGETABLE QUICHE

This quiche is terrific for lunch or dinner if you want a dish that is a change from the ordinary meal routine. The bright colors of the peppers and tomatoes makes it look as great as it tastes. You can use egg substitute equivalent to 4 eggs instead of eggs and egg whites.

PREPARATION TIME:

20 minutes

COOKING TIME:

55 minutes

SERVINGS: *4 – 6*

PIE CRUST

1 puff pastry sheet, thawed for 20 minutes at room temperature *(see Note)*

FILLING

2 tablespoons margarine
1 medium onion, finely chopped
1/2 large green bell pepper, finely sliced
1/2 large red bell pepper, finely sliced
8 medium mushrooms, rinsed and sliced
2 large tomatoes, thinly sliced, divided
2 egg whites
1/4 cup heavy cream
3/4 cup skim milk
1/2 tablespoon dried parsley
2 large whole eggs
Salt and pepper to taste
2 tablespoons Parmesan cheese

Preheat oven to 350 degrees.

PIE CRUST: Smooth out pastry sheet with wet fingertips and line an 8-inch glass pie plate or quiche dish.

Form crust with fingers along top rim of pan to make a neat edge (or get fancy and make scallops). Prick the bottom lightly with a fork and bake for 15 minutes. Remove from oven.

FILLING: While crust is baking, melt margarine in a saute pan or skillet, add onion, peppers, and mushrooms, and cook over low heat until vegetables are just softened.

Arrange onion, peppers, and mushrooms in crust. Evenly place $\frac{3}{4}$ of the sliced tomatoes on top of vegetable mixture.

Beat egg whites until frothy, add cream, milk, parsley, and whole eggs and mix. Pour over vegetables and sprinkle cheese on top. Place remaining tomato slices over all.

Bake for 40 minutes or until top is golden brown. Test by inserting knife into center; if knife is not coated, quiche should be done.

NOTE: To save time, use frozen puff pastry sheets from the freezer section at the grocer (there are two sheets in a box). Don't be intimidated; puff pastry sheets are easy to work with. You can use a pre-formed crust, but I find the type of crust that is unfolded and formed into a baking dish has a much better flavor.

PER SERVING:
Calories: 281
% Calories from Fat: 59
Fat (gm): 19
Saturated Fat (gm): 6.6
Cholesterol (mg): 130
Sodium (mg): 245
Protein (gm): 10.9
Carbohydrates (gm): 18.2

EXCHANGES:
Milk: 0.0
Vegetable: 2.0
Fruit: 0.0
Bread: 0.5
Meat: 1.0
Fat: 3.0

FRENCH TOAST CASSEROLE

This dish always reminds me of a Bed-and-Breakfast on a bright spring day. Your favorite fruit such as fresh blueberries, bananas, strawberries, or golden raisins can be used instead of raspberries.

Vegetable cooking spray
2 cups skim milk
3 whole eggs, lightly beaten, *or use egg substitute*
12 slices wheat, *or whole grain, bread, cut in halves (not diagonally)*
2 tablespoons margarine, melted
$\frac{1}{2}$ cup powdered sugar
2 cups fresh raspberries, *or use frozen if not in season, drained*
1 tablespoon cinnamon

Preheat oven to 400 degrees.

Lightly coat a 9 x 9-inch glass baking dish with cooking spray.

In a small bowl, combine milk and eggs; lightly beat with a fork until blended.

Dip bread halves in egg mixture to coat well. Layer about $\frac{1}{3}$ of slices in bottom of baking dish.

Lightly drizzle $\frac{1}{3}$ of margarine over bread, sprinkle $2\frac{1}{2}$ tablespoons of sugar on top, and cover with half the raspberries or desired fruit. Repeat another layer of bread (pattern differently from bottom layer) and top with $\frac{1}{3}$ of margarine, $2\frac{1}{2}$ tablespoons of sugar, and remaining fruit. Cover with remaining bread, margarine, and sugar. Sprinkle cinnamon over top layer.

Cover and bake for 25 minutes; uncover and bake for an additional 10-15 minutes.

PREPARATION TIME:
15 minutes

COOKING TIME:
35 – 40 minutes

SERVINGS: *6 – 8*

PER SERVING:
Calories: 302
% Calories from Fat: 26
Fat (gm): 9.1
Saturated Fat (gm): 2.1
Cholesterol (mg): 108
Sodium (mg): 416
Protein (gm): 11.8
Carbohydrates (gm): 46.1

EXCHANGES:
Milk: 0.0
Vegetable: 0.0
Fruit: 1.0
Bread: 2.0
Meat: 1.0
Fat: 1.0

STRAWBERRY-BANANA TORTE

Fresh fruit, combined with vanilla pudding, layered between cake strata makes this a delicious addition to any brunch menu.

PREPARATION TIME:

20 minutes

COOKING TIME:

45 – 50 minutes

SERVINGS: **6**

PER SERVING:
Calories: 469
% Calories from Fat: 31
Fat (gm): 16.5
Saturated Fat (gm): 3.4
Cholesterol (mg): 145.8
Sodium (mg): 433
Protein (gm): 11.9
Carbohydrates (gm): 71

EXCHANGES:
Milk: 0.0
Vegetable: 0.0
Fruit: 2.0
Bread: 2.0
Meat: 1.0
Fat: 3.0

Vegetable cooking spray
4 large eggs, *or use egg substitute*
1¼ cups skim milk
2 tablespoons sour cream
4 tablespoons margarine, melted
¾ teaspoon vanilla extract
1⅓ cups flour
1 tablespoon sugar
1¼ tablespoons baking powder
4 fresh ripe bananas, thickly sliced
2 pints fresh strawberries, stems removed and thickly sliced
1 12-ounce container prepared vanilla pudding
¼ cup powdered sugar, for topping

Preheat oven to 350 degrees.

Coat a 9 x 13-inch baking dish with cooking spray.

In a large bowl, combine eggs, milk, sour cream, margarine, vanilla extract, flour, sugar, and baking powder. Using a mixer, blend until very smooth. Pour 1 cup of the batter into baking dish. Bake for about 10 minutes or until set. Remove from oven, but do not turn oven off.

In a large bowl, combine bananas, strawberries, and pudding. Spread half of mixture evenly over baked pastry layer. Pour 1 cup of batter over fruit combination. Carefully spread remaining fruit on top of batter. Pour remaining batter over fruit to cover evenly.

Return baking dish to oven and bake for 45 to 50 minutes or until top is puffed and browned.

Sprinkle with powdered sugar.

EASY CHEESE PUFF

A delicious and fast casserole that tastes like blintzes but requires much less time to prepare. Serve it as a brunch entrée or dessert.

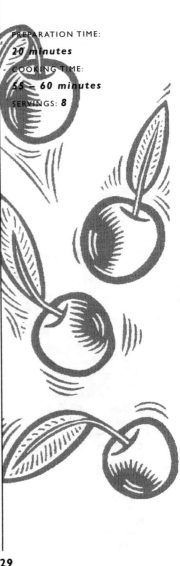

PREPARATION TIME:
20 minutes
COOKING TIME:
55 – 60 minutes
SERVINGS: *8*

PUFF BATTER

    Vegetable cooking spray

4 large eggs, *or* egg substitute

1¼ cups skim milk

2 tablespoons sour cream, *or* plain yogurt

4 tablespoons margarine, melted

¾ teaspoon vanilla extract

1⅓ cups flour

1 tablespoon sugar

1¼ tablespoons baking powder

FILLING

1 pound farmer's cheese, room temperature

1 16-ounce container fat-free ricotta cheese, room temperature

2 large eggs, *or* egg substitute

2 tablespoons sugar

2 tablespoons lemon juice

TOPPING, TO TASTE

    Applesauce

    Strawberries, blueberries, or cherries

    Powdered sugar and cinnamon

Preheat oven to 350 degrees.

Coat a 9 x 13-inch baking dish with cooking spray.

PUFF BATTER: In a large bowl, combine all ingredients for puff batter. Using a mixer, blend until very smooth. Pour 1½ cups of the batter into baking dish. Bake for about 10 minutes or until set. Remove from oven, but do not turn oven off.

FILLING: In a large bowl, combine all filling ingredients and mix well, using a large spoon.

Spread the filling mixture smoothly over the pastry puff in baking dish. Remix the remaining batter and gently pour it over the filling, covering it completely.

Return baking dish to the oven and bake for 45-50 minutes or until top is puffed and browned. Top with desired suggested toppings.

PER SERVING:
Calories: 470
% Calories from Fat: 50
Fat (gm): 26.4
Saturated Fat (gm): 2.8
Cholesterol (mg): 215
Sodium (mg): 577
Protein (gm): 30
Carbohydrates (gm): 29.6

EXCHANGES:
Milk: 0.0
Vegetable: 0.0
Fruit: 0.0
Bread: 2.0
Meat: 2.0
Fat: 5.0

EGG AND BROCCOLI CASSEROLE

It is usually best to use fresh eggs, but for hard-boiling, use eggs that are about three days old. The shells peel better, and the yolks don't turn green.

2 10-ounce packages frozen chopped broccoli, cooked and well drained

4 hard-boiled eggs, peeled and thinly sliced

1 cup reduced-fat sour cream

$1/2$ cup reduced-fat mayonnaise

2 tablespoons tarragon vinegar (if unavailable, use white wine vinegar and $1/2$ tablespoon dried tarragon)

$1/4$ teaspoon paprika

Preheat oven to 325 degrees.

Arrange broccoli in a 13 x 9-inch casserole. Top with egg slices and set aside.

In a small saucepan, over low heat, combine sour cream, mayonnaise, and vinegar, stirring frequently for 4-5 minutes or but do not bring to a boil.

Pour cream mixture over broccoli and eggs; sprinkle with paprika.

Bake, uncovered, 15-20 minutes.

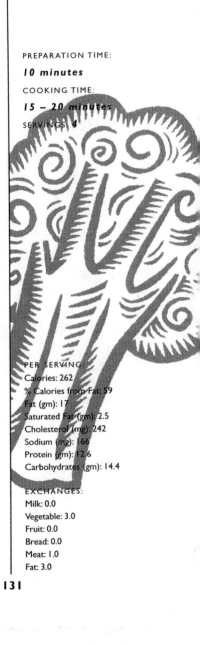

PREPARATION TIME:

10 minutes

COOKING TIME:

15 – 20 minutes

SERVINGS: **4**

PER SERVING:
Calories: 262
% Calories from Fat: 59
Fat (gm): 17
Saturated Fat (gm): 2.5
Cholesterol (mg): 242
Sodium (mg): 166
Protein (gm): 12.6
Carbohydrates (gm): 14.4

EXCHANGES:
Milk: 0.0
Vegetable: 3.0
Fruit: 0.0
Bread: 0.0
Meat: 1.0
Fat: 3.0

dessert delights

Caramelized Apple Casserole

Raspberry Hazelnut Ladyfingers

Berry Crumble Pie

Cherry Strudel

Chocolate Peanut Squares

Pumpkin Custard

Pear Pot Pie

Pineapple Upside-Down Cake

dessert delights

CARAMELIZED APPLE CASSEROLE

Using puff pastry for the top of this dessert makes this a casserole that is light and not too sweet. The pastry sheets are from the freezer section at the grocer (there are two sheets in a box). Don't be intimidated, as puff pastry sheets are easy to work with.

PREPARATION TIME:

15 minutes

COOKING TIME:

30 – 35 minutes

SERVINGS: *6*

6   Granny Smith, *or* other apples for baking, peeled and cut into tenths

½   cup sugar

1   teaspoon cinnamon

1   cup brown sugar *(see Note)*

4   tablespoons margarine, softened

1   puff pastry sheet, thawed for 20 minutes at room temperature

1   egg white, lightly beaten

Preheat oven to 375 degrees.

In a medium bowl, combine apple pieces, sugar, and cinnamon. If you have a lid, cover and shake bowl until apples are well coated or use a spoon to mix together. Set aside.

In a small bowl, combine brown sugar and margarine. Blend with a fork until it is the consistency of small peas. Spread evenly in a 2-quart oval casserole dish.

Spread apples evenly to cover brown sugar mixture.

Unfold puff pastry, smooth out with wet fingertips, and place over apples. Roll out the sheet, if necessary. Tuck excess pastry under, not over, the sides of the dish. Brush top with beaten egg white.

Bake, uncovered, for 25 minutes; increase oven temperature to 400 degrees and continue to bake an additional 5-10 minutes or until golden and puffed.

NOTE: If brown sugar has hardened, place it in the microwave to soften, at 30-second intervals.

PER SERVING:
Calories: 384
% Calories from Fat: 24
Fat (gm): 10.5
Saturated Fat (gm): 1.9
Cholesterol (mg): 0
Sodium (mg): 129
Protein (gm): 1.4
Carbohydrates (gm): 74.8

EXCHANGES:
Milk: 0.0
Vegetable: 0.0
Fruit: 5.0
Bread: 0.0
Meat: 0.0
Fat: 2.0

RASPBERRY HAZELNUT LADYFINGERS

This quick-fix dessert requires hazelnut flavoring. You can use hazelnut liqueur in place of hazelnut-flavored syrup—be sure to tell your guests there is alcohol in it! If you need dessert right away skip the refrigeration and serve immediately.

PREPARATION TIME:

15 minutes

REFRIGERATION TIME:

1 hour

SERVINGS: 6 – 8

1 8-ounce package plain ladyfingers (about 16 fingers)
¾ cup hazelnut-flavored syrup, *or* hazelnut liqueur
3 tablespoons water
1 8-ounce container reduced-fat whipped cream topping, thawed
1 4-ounce container fresh raspberries

Place half of the ladyfingers on a large platter or in a shallow baking dish, arranged nicely. (If you are using a round platter, make a spiral; using a square platter, place evenly in formation—use your imagination.)

In a small bowl, combine hazelnut syrup, or liqueur, and water. Using a tablespoon, spoon half of liquid over ladyfingers.

Spoon half of whipped topping over each finger to cover. Place several raspberries on top.

Arrange remaining fingers on top of raspberries; spoon remaining hazelnut flavoring over ladyfingers. Cover with whipped topping and place several raspberries on top.

Refrigerate for 1 hour. If you have a little whipped topping and some raspberries left over, use them to decorate the empty areas of the platter or dish.

PER SERVING:
Calories: 326
% Calories from Fat: 23
Fat (gm): 8.5
Saturated Fat (gm): 5.9
Cholesterol (mg): 138
Sodium (mg): 70
Protein (gm): 4.8
Carbohydrates (gm): 46

EXCHANGES:
Milk: 0.0
Vegetable: 0.0
Fruit: 2.0
Bread: 1.0
Meat: 0.0
Fat: 2.0

BERRY CRUMBLE PIE

Using fresh berries is the key to this dish. However, if time or season does not permit you to use fresh berries, frozen will work. Just make sure they are thawed and well drained before using.

PREPARATION TIME:

20 minutes

COOKING TIME:

30 minutes

SERVINGS: **6 – 8**

CRUMBLE

- 1 2½-ounce package finely chopped almonds, *or* hazelnuts
- 1½ cups flour
- ½ cup sugar
- 1¼ sticks margarine, slightly softened

FILLING

- ½ cup sugar
- 1½ tablespoons cornstarch
- 2 pints fresh berries (such as raspberries, blueberries, strawberries—use one kind or a combination)

Preheat oven to 450 degrees.

CRUMBLE: In a large bowl, mix together nuts, flour, and sugar. Using a large pronged fork, gradually mix in the margarine to form pea-sized crumbs. Divide and set half of mixture aside.

Using fingers, evenly press half of the crumbles into bottom and sides of an 8- or 9-inch glass tart pan (you can use a regular glass pie pan if necessary).

FILLING: In a medium bowl, mix together sugar and cornstarch. Gently add berries. Spoon coated berries into the crust, spreading evenly.

Sprinkle berry mixture evenly with the remaining crumble topping.

Bake, uncovered, 30 minutes or until top is golden brown and filling is bubbly. Set pan on wire rack to cool for 10 minutes before serving.

PER SERVING:
Calories: 562
% Calories from Fat: 46
Fat (gm): 29.5
Saturated Fat (gm): 5.1
Cholesterol (mg): 0
Sodium (mg): 267
Protein (gm): 6.6
Carbohydrates (gm): 71.1

EXCHANGES:
Milk: 0.0
Vegetable: 0.0
Fruit: 2.0
Bread: 3.0
Meat: 0.0
Fat: 5.0

CHERRY STRUDEL

This Old-World favorite is quick and easy, using ready-made pastry sheets and canned cherries that now come in a very light syrup and taste great. Use frozen puff pastry sheets from the freezer section at the grocer (there are two sheets in a box). Don't be intimidated; puff pastry sheets are easy to work with.

PREPARATION TIME:

10 minutes

COOKING TIME:

15 – 20 minutes

SERVINGS: **8**

PER SERVING:
Calories: 126
% Calories from Fat: 47
Fat (gm): 6.7
Saturated Fat (gm): 1.1
Cholesterol (mg): 0
Sodium (mg): 62
Protein (gm): 1.2
Carbohydrates (gm): 16

EXCHANGES:
Milk: 0.0
Vegetable: 0.0
Fruit: 1.0
Bread: 0.0
Meat: 0.0
Fat: 1.5

FILLING

- 1 15-ounce can pitted cherries in light syrup
- 1/2 teaspoon vanilla, *or almond*, extract
- 1/4 teaspoon ground allspice
- 1/4 teaspoon ground cinnamon

PASTRY

- 2 puff pastry sheets, thawed for 20 minutes at room temperature
- 2 tablespoons margarine, melted
- 1 tablespoon powdered sugar

Preheat oven to 400 degrees.

FILLING: In a medium bowl, mix cherries, vanilla (or almond) extract, allspice, and cinnamon. Set aside.

PASTRY: Unfold one pastry sheet and smooth out with wet fingertips. Brush top with 1/4 of melted margarine.

Spread half of filling along a short side of pastry sheet. Slowly roll up from short side, jelly-roll style; fold ends under.

Place strudel, seam side down, on non-stick baking sheet. Brush with 1/4 of melted margarine.

Repeat using other pastry sheet, remaining cherries mixture, and margarine.

Bake 15-20 minutes until golden. Set baking sheet on wire rack to cool 15 minutes. Transfer strudels to serving platter to cut and serve. Sprinkle with powdered sugar.

CHOCOLATE PEANUT SQUARES

This layered dessert is made fast and easy using your microwave. Make sure you are using bowls that are microwave safe, nothing metal.

I stick plus ½ stick margarine
6 I-ounce squares semisweet chocolate
I cup flaked coconut
I½ cups graham cracker crumbs (about 20 crackers)
½ cup chopped, unsalted peanuts
2 8-ounce packages reduced-fat cream cheese, softened
I cup sugar
I teaspoon vanilla extract

In a medium bowl, microwave 1 stick of the margarine and 2 chocolate squares on high for 1 to 2 minutes or until melted, stirring every 30 seconds. Remove from microwave.

Stir in coconut, graham cracker crumbs, and peanuts. Press mixture onto bottom of 13 x 9-inch baking pan. Place in refrigerator while preparing next layer.

In medium bowl, mix cream cheese, sugar, and vanilla until well blended. Spread over crumb mixture and return to refrigerator while preparing final layer.

In a small bowl, microwave remaining margarine and chocolate on high 1 to 2 minutes or until melted, stirring every 30 seconds. Spread over cream cheese layer. Chill for 1 hour; cut into 14 squares.

PREPARATION TIME:

20 minutes

REFRIGERATION TIME:

I hour

SERVINGS: **14**

PER SERVING:
Calories: 378
% Calories from Fat: 54
Fat (gm): 23.7
Saturated Fat (gm): 7.2
Cholesterol (mg): 11.4
Sodium (mg): 373
Protein (gm): 6.5
Carbohydrates (gm): 38.2

EXCHANGES:
Milk: 0.0
Vegetable: 0.0
Fruit: 0.0
Bread: 2.5
Meat: 0.0
Fat: 4.0

PUMPKIN CUSTARD

By adding pumpkin spice to ordinary custard, you get extraordinary flavor.

PREPARATION TIME:
10 minutes
COOKING TIME:
1¼ hours
SERVINGS: **6**

2 cups skim milk
¼ cup (heaping) sugar
⅛ teaspoon salt
2 whole eggs, beaten
½ teaspoon vanilla extract
1 tablespoon pumpkin spice

Preheat oven to 325 degrees.

In a medium bowl, blend milk, sugar, and salt. Add eggs; beat well. Stir in vanilla and pumpkin spice.

Pour mixture into a 1½-quart casserole. Place the casserole in oven in a pan containing 1 inch of water.

Bake for 1¼ hours or until a knife inserted near the casserole edge comes out clean. Cool on a rack.

PER SERVING:
Calories: 96
% Calories from Fat: 18
Fat (gm): 1.9
Saturated Fat (gm): 0.6
Cholesterol (mg): 72.3
Sodium (mg): 108
Protein (gm): 4.9
Carbohydrates (gm): 14.9

EXCHANGES:
Milk: 0.0
Vegetable: 0.0
Fruit: 0.0
Bread: 1.0
Meat: 0.0
Fat: 0.5

PEAR POT PIE

To save time, use frozen puff pastry sheets from the freezer section at the grocer (there are two sheets in a box). Don't be intimidated, as puff pastry sheets are easy to work with. You can use a pre-formed crust, but I find the type of crust that is unfolded and formed into a baking dish has a much better flavor. Re-roll the leftover dough and cut out leaf and flower shapes to place on top of the crust, making your own design. You still need to cut slits into the crust so steam can escape.

PREPARATION TIME:
15 minutes
COOKING TIME:
30 minutes
SERVINGS: **6**

PIE CRUST

2   frozen puff pastry sheets, thawed for 20 minutes at room temperature
1   egg white, lightly beaten, divided

FILLING

2   tablespoons margarine, softened
¼   cup sugar
½   cup brown sugar *(see Note)*
½   teaspoon cinnamon
¼   teaspoon ground nutmeg
8   fresh pears, peeled, seeded, and cut into eighths

Preheat oven to 400 degrees.

PIE CRUST: Unfold one pastry sheet, smooth out with wet fingertips, roll out, and mold to fit bottom of an 8- or 9-inch pie pan. Form crust with fingers along top rim of pan to make a neat edge (or get fancy and make scallops). Cut three 2-inch slits in bottom of crust to let out steam. Brush with beaten egg white. Bake for 15 minutes or until browned. Remove from oven and set aside. Crust will be puffed, but it will deflate a little as it cools. Reduce oven to 350 degrees.

FILLING: In a medium bowl, combine margarine, both sugars, cinnamon, and nutmeg. Blend with a fork until it is the consistency of small peas. Add pears and mix well. Spread pear mixture to cover baked crust.

Unfold other pastry sheet, smooth out with wet fingertips, and place over pears. Tuck excess pastry inside dish; do not mold around top. With a sharp knife, cut three 2-inch slits into each hemisphere of crust to let steam escape. Brush with beaten egg.

Bake, uncovered, for 25-30 minutes or until golden and puffed.

NOTE: If brown sugar has hardened, place it in the microwave to soften, at 30-second intervals.

PER SERVING:
Calories: 356
% Calories from Fat: 26
Fat (gm): 10.7
Saturated Fat (gm): 1.7
Cholesterol (mg): 0
Sodium (mg): 99.5
Protein (gm): 2.7
Carbohydrates (gm): 67

EXCHANGES:
Milk: 0.0
Vegetable: 0.0
Fruit: 2.0
Bread: 2.0
Meat: 0.0
Fat: 2.0

PINEAPPLE UPSIDE-DOWN CAKE

A traditional dessert in many households. You can't use shortcuts to save time, but you'll see that the effort is well worth it after the first bite.

PREPARATION TIME:
20 minutes
COOKING TIME:
50 minutes
SERVINGS: **10**

TOPPING

    4 tablespoons margarine, melted
    ½ cup firmly packed brown sugar
    1 20-ounce can sliced pineapple, drained
    6 maraschino cherries, halved
    1 tablespoon crushed pecans

CAKE

    1⅓ cups flour
    1 cup sugar
    2 teaspoons baking powder
    ¼ teaspoon salt
    ⅓ cup vegetable shortening
    ⅔ cup skim milk
    1 teaspoon vanilla extract
    1 teaspoon lemon juice
    1 egg, *or* egg substitute

Preheat oven to 350 degrees.

TOPPING: Pour melted margarine into a 9 x 9-inch baking pan. Sprinkle brown sugar evenly over margarine. Arrange pineapple in a pattern over sugar and fill spaces with cherries and pecans. Set aside.

CAKE: In a large mixing bowl, combine flour, sugar, baking powder, and salt; add shortening and milk and beat at lowest speed just to blend. Beat for an additional 2 minutes at medium speed, scraping bowl and beaters once or twice.

143

Add vanilla, lemon juice, and egg; beat 2 minutes longer, scraping bowl occasionally. Pour batter evenly over fruit.

Bake 40-50 minutes or until cake is golden brown and pulls away from sides of pan. Cool on wire rack for 3-4 minutes. Loosen edges of cake and invert onto serving plate, leaving pan in place for 2 minutes before removing. Serve warm or refrigerated.

PER SERVING:
Calories: 338
% Calories from Fat: 32
Fat (gm): 12
Saturated Fat (gm): 2.7
Cholesterol (mg): 21.6
Sodium (mg): 192
Protein (gm): 3.2
Carbohydrates (gm): 55.5

EXCHANGES:
Milk: 0.0
Vegetable: 0.0
Fruit: 2.0
Bread: 2.0
Meat: 0.0
Fat: 2.0

index

A
Artichokes Parmesan, 113
Asparagus
 and Cheese Casserole, 117
 Chicken Oscar, 39
 Roughy au Gratin, 47
 Seafood Newburg, 68
 Spicy Beef and, with Rice
  Noodles, 69

B
Baked Rigatoni, 58
Baked Spanish Rice with
  Cheese, 115
Baked Spinach Mostaccioli,
  98
Baked Taco Dip, 109
Barley Mushroom Bake, 84
Beef
 and Broccoli Teriyaki, 82
 Chili con Carne, 14
 Enchiladas, 19
 Hungarian Goulash, 23
 Pot Roast, 8
 Shish-kabob Casserole, 46
 Spicy, and Asparagus with
  Rice Noodles, 69
 Stroganoff, 67
Beef, ground
 Baked Taco Dip, 109
 Meaty Lasagne, 12
 Noodle Kugel, 59
 Porcupine Peppers, 4
 Rice Dressing, 112
 Shepherd's Pie, 5
 Spaghetti Bake, 89
 Swedish Meatballs, 24

 Tamale Pie, 22
 The Thing, 90
Berry Crumble Pie, 137
Biscuits
 Denver Omelette
  Casserole, 124
 Swiss and Spinach Quiche,
  30
Bread Cubes
 Chicken Oscar, 39
 Fast Ham and Corn
  Casserole, 95
 Zucchini Casserole, 105
Broccoli
 Beef and, Teriyaki, 82
 Caper Chicken with
  Tomato-Basil Linguine, 62
 Casserole, 111
 Chicken Divan, 7
 Egg and, Casserole, 131
 Turkey Bow Tie Pasta au
  Gratin, 64

C
Caper Chicken with Tomato-
  Basil Linguine, 62
Caramelized Apple
  Casserole, 135
Cassoulet au Craig, 26
Cherry Strudel, 138
Chicken
 and Dumplings, 3
 and Noodles, 57
 and Rice Roll-Ups, 73
 Caper with Tomato-Basil
  Linguine, 62
 Coq au Vin (Chicken in
  Wine), 29

 Dijon au Gratin, 79
 Divan, 7
 Garlic and Tri-Colored
  Pasta, 65
 Indian Curry and
  Vegetables, 20
 Jambalaya, 73
 One-Dish and Rice, 99
 Oscar, 39
 Parmesan, 101
 Philippine Pancit, 31
 Pollo Mole (Chicken with
  Brown Sauce), 81
 Quick, and Stuffing, 93
 Shish-Kabob Casserole, 46
 Spicy and Spanish Rice, 78
 Stuffed with Vegetables, 44
 Sun-Dried Tomato
  Couscous with, and
  Mushrooms, 85
 Wild Rice with, and
  Sausage, 83
Chili con Carne, 14
Chocolate Peanut Squares,
  139
Coq au Vin (Chicken in
  Wine), 29
Corn
 Beef Enchiladas, 19
 Fast Ham and, Casserole, 95
 Italian Roll-Ups, 94
 Jambalaya, 73
 Noodle Kugel, 59
 Pollo Mole (Chicken with
  Brown Sauce), 81
 Salmon Soufflé, 50
 Seafood Newburg, 68

Corn (cont.)
  Spicy Chicken and Spanish
    Rice, 78
  Tamale Pie, 22
Corn Bread Casserole, 107
Corned Beef and Cabbage,
    13

D
Denver Omelette Casserole,
    124
Dijon Chicken au Gratin, 79

E
Easy Cheese Puff, 129
Egg and Broccoli Casserole,
    131
Eggs
  and Broccoli Casserole, 131
  Denver Omelette
    Casserole, 124
  Easy Cheese Puff, 129
  French Toast Casserole, 127
  Huevos Rancheros, 123
  Salmon Soufflé, 50
  Spinach Soufflé, 37
  Strawberry-Banana Torte,
    128
  Swiss and Spinach Quiche,
    30
  Tomato and Vegetable
    Quiche, 125
Eggplant
  Layered, and Zucchini Bake,
    41
  Moussaka, 27
  Parmigiana, 60

F
Fast Ham and Corn
    Casserole, 95
Fish
  Asparagus-Roughy au
    Gratin, 47

Salmon Casserole, 38
Salmon, Pea Pod, and New
    Potato Casserole, 48
Salmon Salad, 110
Salmon Soufflé, 50,
Stir-Fry Fish and Vegetable
    Bake, 43
Tuna Casserole, 91
French Toast Casserole, 127

G
Garlic-Cheddar Mashed
    Potato Bake, 114
Garlic Chicken and Tri-
    Colored Pasta, 65
Gravy
  Pot Roast, 8
  Swedish Meatballs, 24
Green Bean Bake, 106

H
Ham
  and Potato Casserole au
    Gratin, 15
  Fast, and Corn Casserole,
    95
  Scalloped and Potatoes, 100
Huevos Rancheros, 123
Hungarian Goulash, 23

I
Indian Curry Chicken and
    Vegetables, 20
Irish Stew, 32
Italian Roll-Ups, 94

J
Jambalaya, 74

K
Kidney Beans
  Chili con Carne, 14
  Wild Rice Casserole, 75

L
Lamb
  Cassoulet au Craig, 26
  Irish Stew, 32
Layered Eggplant and
    Zucchini Bake, 41
Layered Tex-Mex Tortillas, 96

M
Macaroni and Cheese, 9
Meaty Lasagne, 12
Moussaka, 27
Mushrooms
  Baked Rigatoni, 58
  Baked Spinach Mostaccioli,
    98
  Barley, Bake, 84
  Beef Stroganoff, 67
  Broccoli Casserole, 111
  Caper Chicken with
    Tomato-Basil Linguine, 62
  Coq au Vin (Chicken in
    Wine), 29
  Denver Omelette
    Casserole, 124
  Jambalaya, 74
  Pie, 76
  Rice Dressing, 112
  Salmon Casserole, 38
  Spinach Tortellini with, 56
  Sun-Dried Tomato
    Couscous with Chicken
    and, 85
  Tomato and Vegetable
    Quiche, 125
  Veal Scallopini, 42
  Wild Rice Casserole, 75
  Wild Rice with Chicken and
    Sausage, 83
  Zucchini Casserole, 101
  Zucchini Lasagne, 63

N
Noodle Kugel, 59

Noodles
Baked Rigatoni, 58
Baked Spinach Mostaccioli, 98
Beef Stroganoff, 67
Chicken and Noodles, 57
Hungarian Goulash, 23
Macaroni and Cheese, 9
Mushroom-Zucchini Lasagne, 63
Noodle Kugel, 59
Philippine Pancit, 31
Salmon Salad, 110
Spaghetti Bake, 89
Spicy Beef and Asparagus with Rice Noodles, 69
Swedish Meatballs, 24
The Thing, 90
Tuna Casserole, 91
Zucchini Casserole, 101

O
One-Dish Chicken and Rice, 99

P
Pan Pizza Casserole, 92
Pasta
Caper Chicken with Tomato-Basil Linguine, 62
Eggplant Parmigiana, 60
Garlic Chicken and Tri-Colored Pasta, 65
Pork Medallions with Spinach Pasta and Yogurt Sauce, 45
Spicy Tomato Vegetable Linguine, 66
Spinach-Stuffed Shells, 40
Spinach Tortellini with Mushrooms, 56
Turkey Bow-Tie Pasta au Gratin, 64
Veal and Peppers Pasta, 55

Veal Scallopini, 42
Pear Pot Pie, 141
Philippine Pancit, 31
Pineapple Upside-Down Cake, 143
Polenta and Curried Vegetables, 80
Pollo Mole (Chicken with Brown Sauce), 81
Porcupine Peppers, 4
Pork
Cassoulet au Craig, 26
Medallions with Spinach Pasta and Yogurt Sauce, 45
Philippine Pancit, 31
Rice Dressing, 112
Tenderloin with Apricot Stuffing, 49
Pot Roast, 8
Potatoes
Coq au Vin (Chicken in Wine), 29
Corned Beef and Cabbage, 13
Garlic-Cheddar Mashed Potato Bake, 114
Ham and, Casserole au Gratin, 15
Irish Stew, 32
Moussaka, 27
Pot Roast, 8
Salmon Casserole, 38
Salmon, Pea Pod, and New Potato Casserole, 48
Scalloped, 116
Scalloped Ham and, 100
Shepherd's Pie, 5
Sweet Casserole, 108
Puff Pastry
Caramelized Apple Casserole, 135
Cherry Strudel, 138
Mushroom Pie, 76
Pear Pot Pie, 141

Tomato and Vegetable Quiche, 125
Turkey Pot Pie, 10
Pumpkin Custard, 140

Q
Quick Chicken and Stuffing, 93

R
Raspberries
Berry Crumble Pie, 137
French Toast Casserole, 127
Hazelnut Ladyfingers, 136
Rice, Brown
Chicken Stuffed with Vegetables, 44
Indian Curry Chicken and Vegetables, 20
Mushroom Pie, 76
Wild, Casserole, 75
Rice, Long-grain
Jambalaya, 73
One-Dish Chicken and, 99
Pollo Mole (Chicken with Brown Sauce), 81
Wild, with Chicken and Sausage, 83
Rice, Minute
Asparagus-Roughy au Gratin, 47
Baked Spanish, with Cheese, 115
Beef and Broccoli Teriyaki, 82
Beef Enchiladas, 19
Broccoli Casserole, 111
Chicken and, Roll-Ups, 73
Chicken Divan, 7
Dijon Chicken au Gratin, 79
Dressing, 112
Jambalaya, 74
Pork Tenderloin with Apricot Stuffing, 49

Rice, Minute (cont.)
Spicy Chicken and Spanish,
78
Rice Dressing, 112
Ricotta Cheese
Easy Cheese Puff, 129
Italian Roll-Ups, 94
Layered Tex-Mex Tortillas,
96
Meaty Lasagne, 12
Mushroom-Zucchini
Lasagne, 63
Spinach-Stuffed Shells, 40

S
Salmon
Casserole, 38
Pea Pod, and New Potato
Casserole, 48
Salad, 110
Soufflé, 50
Sausage, Turkey
Cassoulet au Craig, 26
Jambalaya, 74
Wild Rice with Chicken
and, 83
Scalloped Ham and Potatoes,
100
Scalloped Potatoes, 116
Seafood
Newburg, 68
Philippine Pancit, 31
Shish-kabob Casserole, 46
Shepherd's Pie, 5
Shish-kabob Casserole, 46
Spaghetti Bake, 89
Spicy Beef and Asparagus
with Rice Noodles, 69

Spicy Chicken and Spanish
Rice, 78
Spicy Tomato-Vegetable
Linguine, 66
Spinach
Baked, Mostaccioli, 98
Baked Rigatoni, 58
Italian Roll-Ups, 94
Soufflé, 37
Stuffed Shells, 40
Tortellini with Mushrooms,
56
Swiss and, Quiche, 30
Stir-Fry Fish and Vegetable
Bake, 43
Strawberry-Banana Torte,
128
Sun-Dried Tomato Couscous
with Chicken and
Mushrooms, 85
Swedish Meatballs, 24
Sweet Potato Casserole, 108
Swiss and Spinach Quiche, 30

T
Tamale Pie, 22
The Thing, 90
Tomato and Vegetable
Quiche, 125
Tortillas
Beef Enchiladas, 19
Huevos Rancheros, 123
Italian Roll-Ups, 94
Layered Tex-Mex, 96
Tuna Casserole, 91
Turkey
Bow Tie Pasta au Gratin, 64
Pot Pie, 10

Turkey, Ground
Rice Dressing, 112
Swedish Meatballs, 24

V
Veal
and Peppers Pasta, 55
Scallopini, 42
Vegetables au Gratin, 118
Vegetables, Mixed
Chicken and Noodles, 57
Garlic Chicken and Tri-
Colored Pasta, 65
Polenta and Curried, 80
Shepherd's Pie, 5
Spicy Beef and Asparagus
with Rice Noodles, 69
Stir-Fry Fish and, Bake, 43
Turkey Pot Pie, 10

W
Wild Rice Casserole, 75
Wild Rice with Chicken and
Sausage, 83

Z
Zucchini
Casserole, 105
Eggplant Parmigiana, 60
Layered Eggplant and, Bake,
41
Mushroom- Lasagne, 63
Spicy Tomato Vegetable
Linguine, 66